Finally Fix Your Credit:

An Insider's Secrets to Getting the Credit Score You Need

2014 Edition

By Boiler Williams, Brad Boruk & Ray Clark

Thank You:

We would like to thank all of the financial and credit insiders, professionals and experts that over the years taught us the importance of managing personal finances along with teaching us the proven methodologies in improving our credit and financial lives.

D1550677

MAY 2015

Boiler Williams, Brad Boruk and Ray Clark:

Finally Fix Your Credit:

An Insider's Secrets to Getting the Credit Score You Need

© 2014, NLA Publishing LLC

NLA Publishing LLC

boiler@NotLegalAdvice.org

Table of Contents

Forward-Testimonials

My name is Curtis and about seven months ago I was having collection problems, a friend of mine introduced me to Boiler Williams who started helping me. Through lots of help and studying I was able to find success in a world filled with collection sharks. Thanks to Boiler and Brad, using their processes I am well on my way to fixing my credit and completely defeating the sharks. I suggest any individual wanting to take the stress and fear out your lives to read and use this book; it will bring lots of satisfaction when you get the results you desire.

From Curtis; Brighton, Colorado

I had horrible credit. I believe it was hurting my ability to get a job. I heard Brad and Boiler on Dallas AM radio talking about fixing people's credit. I didn't call into the radio station that night, but should have. I waited until the next week and listened to their radio show and wrote down their contact information.

The next day I emailed Boiler and later that day talked to Brad about cleaning my credit. I explained that I have tried several times to clean my credit using books by other people. These other processes did not help me.

Brad and Boiler laid out the process that they later put in a book. That process has my credit almost perfect. I did end up getting as new job and they checked my credit. Many thanks to Brad and Boiler!

From Michael; Midland, Texas

Chapter 1
Credit Scores 101
Clearing up the unknown in Credit Scoring

"I got my credit score when I closed on my house last month, it was 726. Yesterday I got my score from the electric company and its 478. How did my score drop so much? Is there something wrong?"

Have you ever experienced this situation or a similar situation? Like many Americans, the credit score is all they hear about when it comes to credit; however, they don't truly understand what the score means. The purpose of this book is to give you a better understanding of scores so that you will better understand how banks, employers, landlords, and others make credit based decisions that will affect your life.

A. The Score

First, let us define a credit score. A **credit score**, simply put, is a numerical reflection of what is contained in your consumer credit report. It is used to predict future events. The meaning of that number is something we will venture into in a bit, but before we do that lets go over the different types of scores. There are three types of scores that banks and lenders may use. There is a **risk score**, which is used to gauge risk for the bank on how likely you are to pay them. That is most likely the score you're most familiar with. The other two types of scores are less common since you may never see one. They are: A **bankruptcy score**, which is used to determine how likely you are to file for bankruptcy, and a **profitability score**, which is used to determine if the entity you are trying to borrow from or are borrowing from is able to make money from the service your applying for or have with them. There may be some other types of scores to gauge other factors but they are far less common.

A.1 Risk Scores

We will start with **risk scores,** as they are the scores you will most likely see and use. Risk for a bank is basically them determining how likely you are to pay them back or make on time payments. It's used to determine future risk based on what is on your credit report at the time it was scored. Being high risk to a bank is having a low credit score. A low credit score is basically saying the bank has less faith that you will pay on time or pay them back. As a result, you may get higher interest rates or be charged a deposit or get denied all together. On the other end, being low risk to a bank facilitates in getting better interest rates and not being charged extra fees and deposits. The benefit is obvious; being less risky saves you money.

So what makes up a risk score? We will get into that in a moment because the answer is not as simple as it might seem. Before we do, let's clarify some misconceptions. Most people assume that because there are three major credit reporting agencies (Equifax, Experian, Trans Union), then you only have three credit scores, one from each agency. That is not actually the case. There are hundreds to thousands of different credit score models. Each bank or lender you apply with has the option to use whichever score model they choose. You could therefore go to bank ABC and apply, they would access your report and grade it 655. You could then go to XYZ bank next door, apply for credit and get a 607. Both banks accessed your same report, but they used different ways to calculate risk. It gives the appearance that the credit score went down but in reality it did not.

An easy way to understand credit scores is to compare them to the temperature. Here in the United States, most people are familiar with and use the Fahrenheit scale to determine if it's jacket weather or not. Let us say you want to take trip to Europe and want to know how to pack. You check the weather in Europe and see that its 36° on the dates that you want to travel. You then decide to pack a heavy coat since 36° is near freezing, right? You board your plane, fly across the ocean, then disembark and realize it is shorts weather. What happened? Was the weather report wrong? The weather report was accurate, Europeans just tell temperature differently. They use the Celsius scale over there. Therefore, if you had actually converted °C to °F you would have known that it was 97° there and packed shorts. You will not be able to convert score models to other score models since you do not have the algorithms used to create them; however, you now know they can be different depending on where you go. The disadvantage to this is that you do not really know what your score is until you apply for credit. The advantage is that since lenders grade you differently, you could get a better interest rate with one lender vs. another. You can also get an approval from a lender for a loan where another would not.

B. What Makes Up a Score?

Now that we know that no two scores are identical, let us delve into what makes up the score. As we stated earlier, scores are made up of what is contained on your credit report. What is on a credit report then? A report contains three parts: your credit cards, loans, other debt, and public records; a list of entities that have looked at your report, more commonly known as credit inquiries; and your personal information (Names and aliases, addresses, employment history, DOB, spouse, and telephone numbers). With respect to your score, the only parts that affect it would be the first two sections mentioned above. Also, with inquiries, only the hard inquiries (inquiries for credit applications) can affect your score. Soft inquiries (When you check your report, account reviews, promotions, and pre approvals) do not. The distinction between hard and soft inquiries on your credit report will be listed. Usually, the different types of credit inquiries are in different sections.

There are five things that a credit score weighs, based on the information found in the report. They are: *payment history*, *amounts owed*, *length of credit history*, *types of credit*, and *new credit*. We have this listed in order of what is weighted greatest to least. You can also look at the chart (FICO Score) to get an idea of how they are weighted with a basic FICO score. We will go over what FICO is further down.

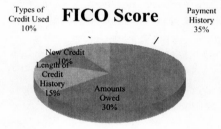

Payment history is usually what the score weighs the most on your report. It includes accounts you've paid on time. Those bring value to your credit score. It will also include any late payments you've acquired, any derogatory items (charge offs, collections, repossessions, etc.), or any public records (bankruptcy, tax lien, civil suit) that may have been filed in the courts. These items may negatively impact your score.

Amounts owed are basically your balances and how they compare to the credit limits or original loan amounts. To increase value here, you'll want to keep your balances as low as possible with you limits as high as possible with respect to your credit cards and other revolving accounts. With loans, just continue to pay your monthly amount due. This will lower the balance and increase the distance from the original amount. Paying off large chunks on an installment loan won't necessarily raise your score. The reason for that is explained next.

Length of credit history is the length of time items on your accounts have been open and active and the length of time since the last activity. The longer an item is on your report and in use, the more valuable it is to you, as long as it is a positively reporting account. Closed or inactive accounts lose their value over time. Therefore, a good account that was opened for 10 years and then closed still helps your score; however, as time passes it helps it less and less. That is why it is important to continually use your credit and be judicious about closing accounts. With regards to amount owed, when paying your monthly payments on an installment loan, you are building positive payment history over the life of that loan. For example: You have a loan for $600 dollars and a term of one year. Keeping it simple we will not do any interest calculations. Your payments come out to $50 a month over the 12 month term. Let us say that you can pay it off in two months. That basically created 2 months of positive payment history. Now the value of that account begins to depreciate since it is paid and closed. On the other hand, if you pay it over the entire term, it shows 12 months of positive payment history before it begins to age. Keep in mind we are just speaking about credit scores and maintaining them. You aren't required to wait the term if you do not want to. This is just to give an understanding of how a lender looks at your information on the report. In most cases, to a lender, paying a loan off more quickly does not look any better to them.

Type of credit is basically your credit mix. Banks and lenders like to see a variety of examples of how you use credit. By having only credit cards on your report, it doesn't give a good picture of how you handle installment loans. It works the other way too. Continually using different types of credit is the best practice here. You want your credit report to look like a decathlete, not just a sprinter or hurdler.

New credit is the last piece of the puzzle. This refers to your new accounts and the credit inquires for new accounts. New accounts do not have any credit history associated with them, so they generally don't add any points. They may actually take some away, since new credit usually includes new debt. Also your credit inquiries factor in. How often you apply for new lines of credit can hurt your score.

You may wonder why that would affect your score negatively. Remember that the score is to calculate risk. Inquiries to a creditor look risky for two reasons: First, depending on how long ago the inquiry occurred, the end result may or may not be on the report. Since the creditor may not know the result of recent inquiries, they are making a decision on unknown information. For example, let's say you apply for a Macy's card. You get the card, make some purchases, and then max it out that same day. A few hours later you apply for a Target card. Target National Bank accesses the credit report and sees an inquiry from Department Store National Bank Macy's. They notice it was done the same day. They don't know that you just maxed out the card. They don't even know if you were approved. That is why the inquiry can hurt your score; the result of it is unknown. The second reason is that multiple inquiries in a short time period may indicate financial duress. If a lender looks at your report and sees you applied at American Express, Bank of America, Discover, US Bank, etc. they may wonder why you need so many accounts in a short period of time. It may be that you just wanted to have an account from each one of those banks, but the lender doesn't know that. To them it looks like you need money immediately. To them it looks more risky and your score decreases.

There are a few fail safes built into scores with regards to inquiries also. You have probably been trying to get a mortgage loan or auto loan and noticed multiple inquiries. Many scoring models take into account when buying a house or purchasing a home that you may need to shop around. For that reason, some models will limit the effect the inquiries will have on the score. They do this by counting them as a single inquiry when within a short time period or weigh it differently.

C. The Scoring Models

Now that we have covered what goes into a risk scores, let us go over a few of the scores you may see or use. We will start with **FICO**. This is the score most people are familiar with. You may have heard that term from a bank when working with them or from a news program covering credit. FICO is an acronym for Fair Isaac & Co. It is basically the name of the company that created it. Fair Isaac & Co actually has over 20 different models. The standard FICO score has a range of 300-850. In most cases this is the score you will be dealing with. It also can be under a few different names depending on which bureaus report it is applied to, namely: **Beacon** on an Equifax report, **Experian Fair Isaac ver. 2** or **3** on an Experian report, and **Empirica** or **FICO Classic** for a Trans Union report. You may see modified versions of the basic FICO also.

Since every lender is different, they may tweak the FICO score to their business needs. Because they may modify the model, the ranges used and the significance of the 5 things that make up the score may be weighted differently. That practice isn't exclusive to Fair Isaac & Co either, most scoring vendors will have the score modified to their clients' needs. Even if two lenders give you a FICO score, they may use different variations of the Fair Isaac's model.
Some other scores you may have seen are **PLUS**, **Vantage 1.0** and **2.0**, and **TEC**. There are actually too many to list. Just keep in mind that every score has a name, the credit bureaus don't track your score, and scores can come from a variety of different sources, not just the bureaus. Now that we understand differences let's transition into score factors.

D. Scoring Factors

Have you ever gotten a denial letter for credit? If you have you know what they look like. If not, let me go over the verbiage of one with you. It goes something like this:

Dear (Your Name),

We regret to inform you that we were not able to open an account with you. The decision we finalized was made in whole or in part from a report obtained from (credit bureau name). You have the right to obtain a credit report from (credit bureau name) within 60 days of this notice.

(credit bureau name)
(credit bureau address)
(credit bureau phone number and website)

Your Score is XXX <may or may not be in the letter>
Factors that adversely affected your score are as follows:
1. *Xxxxxxxxxxxxxx*
2. *Xxxxxxxxxxxxxx*
3. *Xxxxxxxxxxxxxx*
4. *Xxxxxxxxxxxxxx*
5. *Xxxxxxxxxxxxxx*

Sincerely,
{The Lender that denied you}

_____

In the above example, you see the bank used your credit report and used a credit score, but what are the factors mentioned in the letter? Those are called scoring factors. **Scoring factors** are basically reasons why your score is not higher.

There is another misconception we may need to clear up before we get deeper into factors. Most people believe your score starts at the highest number possible in the scoring model used. They also believe that as you miss payments and negative information is added your score decreases. This may also bring them to the conclusion, if they've never missed a payment, they should have a perfect score. That's not actually the case. As we learned when going over what makes a score, scores are not black and white. There is more to them than just missed payments or on time payments. When you start using your credit you have no score. It's not until you have a few accounts on your report that your score can be calculated. As you use credit, add accounts, close accounts, miss payments, etc. your score is calculated and changes depending on the value of these items and the algorithm used.

Now that we know that, let's get back to the scoring factors. What does it mean, "Reasons why the score isn't higher"? Most of the time, you will get four or five factors. Each factor has a value assigned to it. They are listed in order of what is affecting the score the most to what affects it the least. They can have an effect of anywhere from 1 to 100 points against the score.

Unfortunately there is no way to tell exactly how many points each scoring factor is affecting the score. They can also change every time a change occurs on the credit report each time it is scored. On the other hand, they do give you an idea of how you can potentially improve your credit. The factors can give you a starting point of where and how to proceed. Keep in mind those scoring factors are based on what your lender wants to see and the type of score they use, so just as scores are different the factors will be also. This is why you may disagree with the scoring factors at times too. Sometimes they seem a little nitpicky.

Let us say you have an 845 FICO score. Remember the basic FICO score is 300-850, so it is a pretty good score, right? You start looking at the factors and see one that says, "Longest account open is too recent." You think to yourself, "My accounts aren't too recent." Keep in mind that may be true from your point of view, but according to the score's (or the lender you are applying with), it wants more time on the account to get those remaining points. Here are some examples of scoring factors you may see:

Too many inquiries
Longest account opened is too recent
Balance to limit ratio on revolving account is too high
Balance to limit ratio on bank card account is too high
Not enough paid down on real estate accounts
Too many account opened recently
Too many accounts
Not enough accounts
No open bank card account
No open revolving account
Presence of a bankruptcy

That is just to give you a taste, but there are hundreds of different factors you could see. *Scoring factors and scores can also be affected by the amount of data on the report. This works two ways.* Your report is either thick or thin, so the algorithms used into the score will look at the two types of reports differently. It modifies the values of how your payment history, amounts owed, etc. affect the score.

It would seem unfair that the model adapts to how thick or thin your report is, but we have a story to help clarify this. In July 2000 a Concorde jet crashed. This was the first and only crash of the Concorde. Before that crash, Concorde jets were considered one of the safest aircraft based on air miles and flight hours vs. fatalities because no fatalities ever occurred on one. It had a perfect record. After the crash, it became one of the more unsafe jets to travel on and the Concordes were retired shortly after (For the record, the crash was not the only reason for its retirement). The Concorde did not have as many flight hours as conventional jets to help maintain its safety record. Based on the story, a Concorde would be a thin credit report and a conventional jet airliner would be a thick report, since it has more flight hours and miles than its supersonic counterpart.

E. Reporting and Score Accuracy

Now that you know how risk scores work, I want to go over the importance of making sure your report is accurate. As you learned, a good credit score can save you money. For most of us saving money is a good thing. You also learned that a score is a numerical reflection of what is contained in your report, therefore, if your report is wrong then your score is wrong. It is important to check the information on the report. FACTA, an amendment to the FCRA, allows you to request a free report from the credit reporting agencies once every 12 months. Go to annualcreditreport.com or call (877)322-8228 to request yours. Also make sure you are going to annualcreditreport.com as other sites that sound free are not. There are many scams out there even by companies that advertise frequently on TV and say they are free. Remember the reports are free, but the scores the CRAs offer are not. That is ok though, based on what you've learned, that score may not be the same one a bank you're applying with uses.

We also want to touch a little on credit monitoring. Credit monitoring is a tool to track your credit report and have the ability to check the accuracy of it. It also can be used to prevent fraud as you are notified of changes. They also may provide a score and it probably isn't the score a bank will use, but it gives you a way to see what your credit is doing. You're able to track the score they provide you and see which direction your credit is moving, positively or negatively.

Since you are able to track a score with monitoring you may also see the score will fluctuate. Keep in mind your report is not a static document therefore the score is not either. It is normal for your score to increase and decrease a few points within a months' time. Your balances and payments are not all reported at the same time which means as data is modified and changed at different times, your score will also change accordingly. Large leaps are what you will want to look for. If you are tracking your score with a service, it may also be a good idea to save the reports. Pinpointing the reason for a score change is difficult if you do not know what the report looked like before. If you have a score change you can look at the old report and compare it to the new one to see what is different. The differences will indicate why the score may have changed.

F. The Other Scores

The information we have just covered applies to risk scores. Fortunately, much of it also applies to bankruptcy scores and profitability scores. You may never see a bankruptcy or profitability score, but lenders are using them just as much as risk scores. You may even feel the effects of them and not know it.

Here is a scenario that happened to someone we know. This is the best example we have on how a **profitability score** is used. This person had very good credit. Their score was over 800 with the basic FICO model. They had a Wachovia Bank card back when Wachovia was still in business. The bank card was very nice because the interest rate was around 5%. Wachovia sold their bank card accounts to Bank One. Bank One sent them a letter after purchasing the account. The letter was similar to a denial letter. It basically stated that they had to increase the interest rate to 20% because of the credit report. This person was furious. They wondered what could have happened to their report to make Bank One react like that.

They obtained the free report and nothing was wrong. What actually happened is when Bank One bought the accounts, they did what is called an account review inquiry (Which shows up as a soft inquiry on the report and does not affect the score). Based on the credit report and this person's spending habits, they determined, a bank card at 6% would not be profitable for them. This probably sounds unfair, but remember, a bank is a business and by nature it is designed to make money.

Now we are going to give you a scenario to better understand a **bankruptcy score**. You have lost your job and your budget is stressed because you have less money coming in. To compensate you start using your credit cards more to extend your savings until you find new employment. You notice your balances are getting close to your credit limits. You continue to make your payments on time and are not too worried about it because you have some good job leads. You get your mail a little later and notice a mundane envelope from your bank card issuer. You open it and it is a letter similar to the denial letter above, except it says your account has been closed. Confused you call the issuer to find out what happened as you have not missed a payment with them. They tell you there is a problem with your report.

You're now stressed out because you have just been told there is something wrong with your credit report. You obtain a copy of the report and everything is as it should be. The balances are high, but you already knew that. What happened then? The bank did an account review for your report. The used their bankruptcy score model and it determined that there was a high probability that you might declare bankruptcy. The bank did not want to take the risk you might declare bankruptcy, so they closed your account so that you could not borrow more. By doing this, if you did declare bankruptcy they would only lose what you have already used and not anymore. Again, probably not fair, but a bank is business.

In conclusion, we now know a modern lender uses various score types and score models to make decisions. These models are based off of the information that can be scored on the credit report. There are many types of scoring models and to compare them would be like comparing apples to oranges. You have three credit reports, one from each credit reporting agency, but there are hundreds of ways they can be graded. It is important to check the accuracy of the report to make sure you get the most out of your score. And a final note, a good score can save you money, so keep up with it.

Chapter 2
The Credit Report
What's in it?

There are many misconceptions of what is found in a credit report. Many people do not know what is contained in one or where they come from. In fact, many Americans have not even seen theirs. We are going to explore the credit report, so that you have a better grasp of what is contained in them and what's not. We will also look at where they came from and how they are compiled. Read on and most of your questions about credit reports will be resolved.

A. The Credit Agencies

Let us start with where a credit report comes from. There are five major credit-reporting agencies. They are *Experian*, *Equifax*, *Trans Union*, *Innovis*, and *PRBC*. Of the five, you normally only need to concern yourself with Experian, Equifax, and Trans Union. They are known as the "Big Three" credit bureaus. Innovis and PRBC are not at par and contain less information than the other three. A *credit-reporting agency*, for all intents and purposes, is an information storage company. They collect information about you, submitted by companies you do business with, in the form of credit related transactions. This information is then stored, maintained, and sold by these companies. The information they collect is called your credit report. Since there are multiple companies collecting data about you, you have more than one credit report. You have one from each company. These credit reports are similar but not identical. We will look at why that is further down.

Now that you know what they do, you are probably wondering how they collect information about you and when it started. Your credit report is first created when you apply for credit, the first time. When you apply for credit, that lender you applied with will contact the agency they do business with and ask for the credit report they have on you. If that credit agency has no information on you, it creates a new file and sends it to the lender. A new credit report is then created and will only contain the information that the lender submitted when he/she requested the report. As you use credit, your lenders that work with that agency will submit their information to them and your credit report grows.

The reason why your credit report varies from one credit-reporting agency to another is that not all banks and lenders will do business with each other. As an example, a loan from your local federal credit union may report to Equifax, but they may not to Experian or Trans Union. While your cellular phone may only access a Trans Union report to assist in their decision making process. Since banks and lenders choose whom they work with, it causes differences in your credit reports. Most entities you borrow from will report to all three credit-reporting agencies though.

B. Parts of the Credit Report

Now that we know where these reports come from, let us touch on what is included in one. Your credit report is divided into 3 sections. They are: *personal information*; *credit, loan, and debt information*; and *credit inquiries*. We will expound on each section.

B.1 Personal information

It is exactly what it sounds like. Its information used to identify you. It includes names, addresses, phone numbers, employment history, Social Security numbers, and spouse or co-applicant name, and variations of that information.

B.1.a Names

These are the names and aliases associated with the items on your report. If your credit card has a name of John J Smith III, then that name will be on your credit report. If another card has the name JJ Smith III, that will also be on the report. Whatever variation of spelling on any credit card, loan, or other debt, it will show up on the report. This includes typos and misspellings. We will tackle how to fix these mistakes in a bit. The main point here is that your report does not just have one name; it has all the names used to establish credit, submitted by your lenders.

B.1.b Addresses

On a report, addresses are not necessarily the places that you have lived in the past, they are billing addresses. Any place that you have set up as a billing address will show up on your report. For example, you find it easier to receive mail at work. You change the addresses on all your credit cards so that you receive statements at work. The credit card issuers will update your report and add your work address to it. You do not live in your workplace, but the address will show up as long as it is the billing address of each of your credit accounts. If you decide to change the address back to your home address to receive statements, you will be able to have your work address removed.

Here is another scenario where you may see an address you have not lived in on your report. You and your sister cosign for a loan. You both decide that she will receive the statements. Her address is now on your report. A very common error in this section is a mistyped zip code. This causes problems when the zip code is for another area or state. If your zip code is 40210 you're from Louisville KY. If a 4 is mistaken for a 9, you're now from Beverly Hills CA. Be aware also that incorrect addresses may be related to fraud or merged files. We will cover those shortly.

B.1.c Employment History

Your **employment history** is just a listing of where you have worked or are currently working. It is probably one of the least updated parts of your report. Usually, this section is updated whenever you apply for new credit. When you fill out the credit application, it has a section for employment. When the lender you are applying with submits the report request, they may add your employment information. Your employer does not add this information. It is modified when you apply for credit or when you contact the credit bureau and add or update it.

B.1.d Social Security numbers

These are listings of the Social Security numbers used, related to your credit items. You may have noticed the words Social Security numbers is in plural form. That is not a mistake. I know you are thinking you only have one. You are right. Unfortunately, mistakes happen. Creditors submitting data can mistype information. The person entering it may push the wrong digit on the 10key or read your handwriting wrong on a handwritten application. These mistakes add variations of your SSN to the report. Like the rest of the report, these errors can be corrected.

B.1.e Spouse or co-applicant name

This is the name of the first person you ever co-signed an account with. For most people this is your spouse. This hardly updates unless you notice it is wrong. The most common mistake with this is when it is an ex-spouse.

The personal information on the report is usually where most people notice mistakes. The reason for that is this is the information most familiar to you. For that reason, most disputes are related to the personal information section. To reduce the amount of disputes received, credit-reporting agencies may order the personal information section last. Do not overlook this section. Even though it does not affect your score, it can affect other factors with regards to obtaining credit.

B.2 Credit, Loan and Other Debts

Your *credit, loan, and other debts* section is usually the largest section of your report. It will most likely be the first section you see when you open it up. It includes all your credit cards and loans. It may also include collection accounts and public records. This section can be broken into two subsections: your credit that negatively impacts your score and that which positively impacts your score.

Your information that is considered potentially negative, are public records and any credit that has reported late payments. There are three types of *Public records* and they include bankruptcies, tax liens, and civil actions. Other types of public records are not part of your credit profile. You will not see arrest records or divorce records on your report.

B.2.a Bankruptcy

This is a status of a person who is unable to pay their creditors. It is filed through the federal court systems and is therefore a public record. It falls under different chapters, but the most common chapters seen on a consumer credit report are Chapter 7 and Chapter 13. More on bankruptcy later in this book, but as far as your credit is concerned, here are the specifics.

Chapter 7 bankruptcy is when the debtor is absolved of all of their debts (except debts protected from bankruptcy i.e. Federal backed student loans). This type of bankruptcy can remain on a credit report for up to ten years from the date filed.

Chapter 13 bankruptcy happens when the borrower is set up in a payment plan to pay back a portion of the debt owed. This type of bankruptcy can remain on a report for up to seven years from the date filed.

The chapter type of bankruptcy filed will affect your score in the same manner; both will affect it negatively. The only difference on how it affects your credit report is the retention time. On your report you will see the chapter filed and the bankruptcy status. The status is the stage your bankruptcy is in. It can be under petition, dismissed, or discharged and these are defined below:

- *Petition* means you started the bankruptcy proceedings.
- *Dismissed* signifies either you decided not to go through with the bankruptcy or the courts denied your request.
- *Discharged* means that you have completed the bankruptcy.

B.2.b Tax liens

These are unpaid taxes that have been filed in the court system. These liens can be filed at the local, state, and federal level. This is the item that has the potential to be on your credit report longer than any other item. A tax lien can stay on a report for ten years from the filing date or seven years from the date paid. This means that if you paid a lien in 2013, which was filed in 2004, it has the potential to stay on your report until 2020. A paid tax lien shows as satisfied. Withdrawn or dismissed liens should not appear on your credit report.

B.2.c Civil actions

These are law suits. These are not suits waiting for a court date or cases without a verdict. These are lawsuits that you, as a defendant, have lost. They stay on your credit report for seven years from the date filed regardless if paid or not. Withdrawn or dismissed suits should not be on your credit report.

Now that we have covered public records, let us get to the rest of your potentially negative information. We are going to first define the types of accounts in this section, because you will also see these in your positive section. They are revolving accounts and installment accounts.

Rent and utilities are not included in these categories. They may appear though, if you default on either, usually as a collection account. Further down, collection accounts will be explained.

B.2.d Revolving Accounts

These are your accounts that have no set terms for a payback schedule. You are just required to pay a percentage of the balance when the payment is due. Some payment periods may not have a balance so no payment will be due. You are also able to borrow repeatedly as long as you are under the established credit limit. The most common account you will see of this type is a credit card. These accounts will report the date opened, date of last reporting, date of last activity, credit balance, minimum payment, credit limit or original balance if no limit is reported, high balance and your payment history.

B.2.e Installment Accounts

This differs from revolving accounts in that they have a set payment schedule and the original amount borrowed cannot change. Car loans, home loans, and personal loans fall into this category. These accounts will report the date opened, date of last reporting, date of last activity, credit balance, monthly payment, original balance, high balance, and your payment history.

Here is something to get you thinking. Original balance and high balance are mentioned because in most cases, those amounts will be the same, but there are instances where they are not. So when would the high balance be above the original balance? If you said missed or deferred payments, you are correct. Missed or deferred payments still accrue interest and could raise your current balance above the original balance. It was mentioned above that the amount borrowed does not change. This may have triggered the question, "What about refinancing?" Refinancing is the opening of a new loan in place of the previous. The bank does not restructure the current loan. It creates an entirely new one. On your report you will see the old loan as paid and closed. The new one will be open in its place.

So where is the negative factor in this section? It is the payment history associated with your revolving and installment accounts. Any late payments from **30 days to 150 days** can be considered negative. There are other statuses in the payments history that can be considered negative and are also classified as derogatory statuses. These are:

- ***180 days late-*** is an account delinquent for over 6 months
- ***charge off-*** a debt written off by the lender, for accounting and tax purposes;
- ***repossession-*** an account involving property transferred back to the lender because of missed payments or loan default
- ***voluntary surrender*** - an account involving property transferred back to the lender, initiated by the borrower
- ***foreclosure-*** real estate property being transferred to the lender, because of missed payments or loan default, and occupants are evicted
- ***foreclosure proceedings started*** - borrower initiating steps to take over the real estate property because of missed payments or loan default
- ***defaulted on contract*** - the debt or contract obligation is in default or has not been fulfilled
- ***paid by creditor*** - the debt was paid by the creditor when in default
- ***insurance claim*** - debt covered by and paid by insurance company
- ***claim filed with government*** - debt backed by the government was transferred to the government and lender received payment from the government
- ***creditor received deed*** - creditor received deed of property because of missed payments or loan default
- and ***collection*** (see below).

You will also see accounts included in bankruptcy and settlement areas. The negative reporting can only stay on your report for seven years from the first reported missed payment by the original creditor. Some people confuse the seven year time period with the open date, but the open date has no bearing on the accounts' retention time.

Here is how it works. Let us say you missed a series of payments on your Diner's Club card in 2005. You missed June, July, August, and September. For each month you missed, Diner's Club reported 30, 60, 90, and 120 days late. The first missed payment then is June 2005. You add 7 years to that date and voila, the late payment history is removed by June 2012 and the account retains the positive history. Keep in mind, any late payments reported older than seven years, should not appear on your report. It is 2013 so anything from 2006 will come off during this year. Anything that goes into derogatory status will be completely removed after the seven year period. That also includes the accounts included in bankruptcy and the settled accounts.

B.2.f Collection accounts

These are accounts that are late and have either been transferred to their collections department or sold to a collection company. They are treated as installment accounts on the report. Most of the time you will see the account in the collection company form.

A **collection company** is an organization that purchases accounts with the purpose of making a profit on receiving payments for those accounts. You may wonder how they can make a profit on collecting if the balance is no different from that of the original creditor. They purchase these accounts in bulk at a significantly discounted rate. Collection companies often pay 4 to 7 cents on the dollar for debt. They hope that when they receive payment, it will be at the full balance. That is how they turn a profit.

You may also see these accounts on your report and believe them to be duplicates of the original creditor. They are not duplicates. They are within their rights to add the account to the report if it is a valid debt. You will notice that the open date is different than the original creditor. This does not change the seven year retention period for the debt. This account is required to come off the same month as the original creditor's reported first late payment. It is against the law for them to modify this date or re-age the account. Watch for this. If you notice the original creditor was removed and the collection account is still there, this is probably an error and needs to be rectified.

B.2.g Settled Accounts

These are accounts which you and the creditor have agreed on a payoff amount. These amounts are less than the full balance. It shows on the report as legally paid for in full for less than full balance. It can also be considered negative. A short sale with a mortage falls into this category also. The reason it may be considered negative is that the original contract was not fulfilled.

Now as far as **positive accounts** or **accounts in good standing** go, they are basically your credit cards, loans, and other debts with no late or derogatory payment history associated with them. The information above about revolving and installment loan accounts pretty much covers them. I do not think we need to go back into them.

Next we have credit inquiries. The **credit inquiries** is the section which contains a listing of all the entities that have requested a copy of your credit report. These requests are maintained on the credit report by the credit reporting agencies for a minimum of two years. By two years they usually fall off automatically. I will go over credit reporting errors in a bit to give insight into how to correct the report if you see some old inquiries. Your inquires are divided into two sub sections, soft inquiries and hard inquiries.

Soft inquiries are inquiries that will not affect your credit score. Creditors are not able to see this section but you are. These can be requests for the report from you. When you look at your own report, it records as an inquiry. The company you used to access the report then appears on the report in this section. Other reasons for soft inquiries are: account reviews, pre-approvals, employment, insurance, and utilities. You will probably see account reviews more than any other type here.

Account reviews are when a creditor you currently have an account with is checking your report to potentially modify your terms or continue with your current terms. Some creditors do this monthly so you can see quite a few from a lender. Have you ever received mailings for credit card or loan offers? Those mailings are part of the *pre-approval* process. Creditors will access your credit information, and if they like what they see; they send an offer. Again, these do not affect the credit score, but some people do not like receiving these offers. If you call (888)5-OPTOUT or (888)567-8688, you can be removed from the lists the credit bureaus sell for pre-approvals. Calling that number only removes you temporarily. To do it permanently you must respond to the letter they send you after you call in.

Hard inquiries have the potential to affect your credit score. Most of these are related to when you apply for credit. When you apply, the company you apply with will access you report and the inquiry is then recorded. The other reason for a hard inquiry is when a company is purchasing a debt from another. They may access your report to see if they want to purchase it. These are far less common than then the inquiries related to you applying. Since they can affect your score it is recommended you be judicious about applying for credit.

C. Errors in Reporting

Now that you know what a report contains, we will cover reporting errors. The credit reporting agencies are required to maintain accurate credit reports of the people in their databases. Unfortunately, these companies are not perfect in their data maintenance. The Consumer Data Industry Association claims 98% material accuracy on the reports. 98% sounds very good, doesn't it?It's like getting a 4.0 average in college. Consider this though. There are 238 million adults over 18 years of age. Assuming the all have applied for credit at least once, that comes out to around 5 million errors. Another study from the Federal Trade Commision states that there are close to 40 million errors in credit reporting. Either way, millions of errors is not a good thing, especially if it is your credit report. Fortunately we have the right to dispute the errors contained in the reports. Unfortunately it can be a daunting task. Of all the parts we have gone over though, each one is disputable. There are three types of errors you may find on your report. They are: inaccuracies from your creditors, database errors from the credit agency, and credit fraud.

C.1 The Creditor Submits Inaccurate Information

The most common error is the first one mentioned. The **creditor submits inaccurate information**. I have mentioned some of the errors in some of the information we covered above. Most of those mentioned above would fall into this category. Most of these types of errors will be in your personal information section. Those would mostly be typos in names, addresses, employment, etc. Fortunately those will not hurt your score. They can impact application screening though. A bank accesses your report and compares it to your application; if they see discrepancies they may instantly deny your application. This also can make it difficult to get your own credit report. If the credit report contains misinformation, when you ask for one with your correct information, the agency will not give you your report. They will then require you to do everything in the mail. In the fast paced society we live in, mail seems very slow. So even if it does not affect the score, it is important to make sure it is correct. The other errors submitted by your lenders will affect your score. If they report an incorrect credit limit or a late payment, when you were not late, that would hurt your ability to get credit. Some lenders may even report you as deceased. When accounts reported as deceased are on your report, you cannot even get a score. It is an immediate denial. Make sure to check each item thoroughly to make sure thay are accurate.

C.2 Database errors

These are errors caused by the systems the credit agencies use to keep your information. These are seen as split credit files and merged credit files. **Split credit files** are when your credit report is divided into two or more reports. These can be triggered by a mistake by the lender, but most of the time its an error in the credit reporting agency's software. It is caused when the database software fails to recognize the information submitted and creates a new credit report. Sometimes a change of address can trigger this or a spelling of the name.

For example: A person named William has used his name on his credit applications for years. To his friends he is Bill. He wants to get a new loan and he has a friend who is a banker. He goes to the bank and applies. His banker friend fills out the application using Bill. The SSN and address are the same as always. The credit agency returns a credit report that is nearly blank. In this case, the credit agency's system thought William and Bill were two different people and created a new credit profile. Taking it one step further, let us say William got approved. The new account would be on the Bill version of the report. If he applies for different loans at that point forward, depending on the name used, the banks will be looking at two different reports. If you see items missing or feel your report is incomplete your credit report may be split.

C.3 Merged credit files

There are times when your credit file is shared with another consumer. This is another identification error in the agency's data base software. Here is how this works. For this example we will use a father and son combination. We will use Thurston Howell III and his son Thurston Howell IV. Before Thurston Howell III sails off on the S.S. Minnow and gets stranded on a tropic isle, he wants to have his son establish credit. They go to the bank and apply. Thurston Howell IV gets a new credit card with an extremely low interest rate and a very high limit. How did the 4th get such a good interest rate and high limit? The bank picked up the 3rd's report in this case.

The credit agencies database assumed that was the report they wanted since the names and addresses matched. They didn't make a new credit file for the 4th like they should have. Now any credit the 4th goes after and gets will be added to the 3rd's report. It does not seem too bad, right? Well here is the next part of the story. We know that Thurston Howell III got rescued from the tropic isle at least twice in made for TV movies. He needs to re-establish himself after being rescued. He applies for new credit and gets denied. How could this happen? He is Thurston Howell III, he is "The Millionaire." Well Thurston Howell IV has not been paying his bills since his father went missing. Because they share the report, the 4th's bad credit is mixed with the 3rd's good credit. If you do not recognize names, addresses, or accounts, good or bad, your credit report maybe merged with another person's.

C.4 Credit Fraud

Credit fraud is technically not an error, but signs of it look similar to errors on your report. It is also something that will most likely harm your credit . **Credit fraud** is when someone impersonates you, using your identifying information, to open lines of credit. It is a form of identity theft.

Indicators of this will be similar to a merged credit file. In a merged file you may see variations of names and addresses similar to yours. With fraud you will also see that or completely foreign addresses from other states. You will also see accounts you do not recognize and inquiries for credit you did not apply for, just like on a merged file. The difference here is that a merged credit file may contain positive accounts. With fraud, the accounts will most likely be maxed out and no payments attempted.

If your credit file looks correct, yet you start to notice strange inquiries, that would also be an indicator you may be a victim of identity theft. If you see these types of errors, you will want to take action immediately. Remember you are the victim in this case. You are not responsible for debts on your credit report that are related to fraud.

D. Correcting the Report

You are now familiar with the report and the errors contained in it. Your are now wondering how to fix these errors. There are various ways to do that. You can do it yourself or you can hire a company or organization to do it for you. We recommend Brad's company National Credit Solutions (www.ncs700.com). Either way the first step is getting your credit report and identifying the errors. Once you pinpoint the errors its time to start the fixing process. I will begin with explaining the credit report dispute process.

D.1 Credit Report Dispute

A *credit report dispute* is when you contact the credit agencies and question the accuracy and validity of an item. The credit agencies then contact the data furnisher. They ask them to verify the information, then the report gets updated accordingly. The *data furnisher* is the creditor whose account you are questioning. They provide the data for the report. The data furnisher must reply within 30 (17 for residents of Maine) days or less. If they do not respond, the item gets updated in favor of how you disputed it. The 30 day (17 day for Maine) time limits changes to 45 days (21 for Maine) when disputes are filed based off of your free annual credit report (I will explain how to get that in a moment).

Sounds easy, right? Unfortunately, verifying information to you or me means something different to the credit agencies. They do not usually contact the creditors directly. They use an electronic system named *E-Oscar* to verify accounts. This saves time in the disputing process, but does it really verify the accuracy? I will let you be the judge of that. It is our belief that all 3 of the big credit reporting agencies violate federal law (Fair Credit Reporting Act) when verifying issues on a credit report. Regardless, here is how it really works. A person contacts the credit agency and tells them they were not late on their credit card. The credit agency submits the dispute to the E-Oscar system in the form of codes the system understands. Then the creditor(data furnisher) is notified the item is being disputed through the E-Oscar system and reviews the codes sent from the credit agency. The creditor sends back a set of codes to respond, based on their records. E-Oscar sends the response codes to the credit agency and the report is modified based on those codes. Most of this is done electronically. Little or no human interaction is required for this process. No documents were researched and no signatures verified. Was the person really late on the account or not? That is one of the hurdles in the dispute process. Little human interaction can make you question the validity of an investigation. For entities that do not use E-Oscar, the credit agencies send mailings to them that they are required to respond to. The mailings include the dispute reasons and request a response for the furnisher by mail. Mail does go through more human hands, but it is a fading method of contact with the speed and efficiency of E-Oscar. E-Oscar's efficiency helps add to profitability, but the system does little to verify consumer disputes.

D.2 Proof Documents

Credit agencies will also accept documents that support your dispute. These are referred to as **proof documents**. Proof documents can be anything from a bill, release from the courts, bankrupcy schedule, a letter from the creditor, or anything else that supports your dispute. If sending in proof documents to a credit agency, never send the original because you may never see it again. The benefit to sending documents is that the agency can update and correct the account based on the information on your document. The drawback to this is that even if a document is valid and the person reviewing the document at the credit agency questions that validity, they will most likely file the dispute through the E-Oscar system.

D.3 Phone Verification

Phone verification is one option to get errors cleared up. This is when you speak to a dispute agent and they contact the data furnisher with you to verify the validity of an item you are questioning. The benefit to this is that you get an instant solution... pending the phone hold times are short. The shortcoming of calling is that you do not create a documentation trail that can later be used should litigation arise.

Here is a scenario to explain the benefits of phone verifying. A consumer notices an account that is not theirs. It is a good credit account. Most people overlook positive accounts, but they can be mistakes also. They dispute it by mail. The E-Oscar process takes place. A few weeks later the consumer gets an update that states the account is verified and is theirs. They try again. He gets the same response. They are now angry and decide to call. The dispute agent they contact looks at the account and sees the item has been disputed multiple times for the same reason. To assist the angry consumer the agent calls the data furnisher with them. They wait on hold and get transferred a few times. They finally get to someone who can assist them. The agent at the data furnisher notice the mistake. The owner of the account has the same name as the consumer but a different SSN. The data furnisher merged their data which caused an error on the credit report. The data furnisher reported the wrong information on the account and the account was then put on the wrong report. If the agent at the credit agency had not phone verified the account, it may have never been rectified.

Public record disputes work differently than standard credit disputes. You dispute them the same way as you would a credit account. The difference is in the background. The credit agencies do not actually contact the courts individually when you dispute a public record. They use data furnishers that specialize in public records. These data furnishers are basically companies that have a data base of public records that the credit agencies purchase. The agencies then add that information to the credit report. These data furnishers, just like with credit accounts, can use E-Oscar. You can also send in proof documents from the courts or have an agent at the credit agency phone verify directly with the court the public record was filed in.

I just want to bring to light an issue with the way public records are reported and disputed. Using a third party to maintain the credit reporting agencies' public record information could cause errors in your report. There are thousands of courts across the country. You have city courts, county courts, state courts, and federal courts. They depend on this third party to stay up to date with its information. If your tax lien gets withdrawn and this third party never updated; when you dispute it, the item will remain on your report. Public records also do not contain SSNs. This could cause merged credit file issues. Kate Smith and Katie Smith live in the same apt complex. There names are similar, they were both born in 1984, and they live in units 104 and 304. Since there is not an SSN to help distinguish the two of them, the probability that they become merged increases. Kate's bankruptcy could show up on Katie's otherwise spotless credit report.

You know the signs of merged and split credit files. If you think your file is merged or mixed, be specific in your correspondence. Agents at the credit reporting agencies are not trained to look for merged and split files. They are just trained to enter your dispute and submit. If you are not specific with the issue you have, they will not look for it. Here is an example of how they are trained. You write in about a late payment a lender told you about when you applied for a loan. You have credit monitoring and have never seen that. The agent at the credit agency opens your letter, looks up your file and does not see the account either. You get a letter back stating the account is not on file and to review your report. How does the bank see this account that you and the credit agency cannot see? Its because it is a split credit file. Ask them to do a SSN search and see if your SSN is divided on multiple files. If they do that they will see it is split and take the steps necessary to correct it. Use words like split, divided, mixed, and merged to help them along.

D.4 Fraud Disputes and Fraud Alert

Fraud disputes the same way also. I recommend taking extra steps when you are a victim of credit fraud. You have seen how E-Oscar works. So if you just dispute a fraud, since the identity thief impersonated you, they will not remove the items. The creditor has no way to distinguish you from the fraudster.

With fraud you will first want to add a fraud alert to the credit report. A **fraud alert** is a notification to creditors, that you are or may have been a victim of fraud, and for them to contact you if new applications for credit are submitted in your name. The initial alert will last for 90 days. You are also able to obtain a free report if you add this alert. This will help stop any new fraudulent items from being added to the report. If you add it on any agency, it will be added to all of them.

The next step would be to access your report, if you have not already. Once you have identified the fraud, obtain a police report. You will then want to contact each company on your report and let them know of the fraud, so that they know it was not you opening or attempting to open the accounts. They may request additional information from you, like the police report you filed. Do not worry yourself about asking the creditors who committed the fraud against you. You will be curious, but they will most likely refuse your inquiry and only deal with police after you have reported the fraud to them. They will not know much more anyway; they thought it was you using their services.

Once you have dealt with the creditors, submit your disputes to the credit agencies. Send a copy of your police report with the disputes. You can also extend your fraud alert to seven years if you choose. All you need to do is request they extend it when you send in your police report. Again, you are not responsible for the monies stolen from these lenders because of credit fraud. If they ask you to pay them, do not oblige. This is a tactic they may use for you to take responsibility for the debt.

If you obtained a police report and sent it to the credit agencies, you can also add a credit freeze, free of charge. A *credit freeze* is a type of lock for your credit profile. It prevents any entity not on your credit report from looking at it. Your report will either need to be unfrozen to be accessed by a creditor or you will need to obtain an access code for them to access it. The freeze should not prevent you from accessing your own report.

E. Getting your report

You are now familiar with the credit reports, the companies that create them, fraud and errors, and how to dispute and make corrections. The whole system can be frustrating and daunting. Especially when you get denied from a lender and it is for reasons that are not your fault. Keep up with your credit report. You can use credit monitoring or buy a single report. There are free available options too. Some states offer free reports. Check with your state government to see if you qualify. You also have the right to obtain a free report once every twelve months. Go to http://www.annualcreditreport.com or call (888)322-8228. You can also write directly to each agency and ask for the free annual report. As I stated above, you can also get your report if you feel you may have been a victim of identity theft and credit fraud. Contact each agency and add an alert to obtain a free report. You can also write in with proof that you are currently receiving public welfare assistance or are unemployed to get a free report. Also if you receive adverse action you can obtain a free copy. *Adverse action* is when a a lender, utility, or insurance company denies you services or gives you an unsatisfactory interest rate, or changes your terms based on information on a credit report. If you've received an adverse action letter, send it to the credit bureau used to get your free report. My final words to you are a repeat of what I said earlier, keep up with your credit report. Make sure your report is accurate and up to date, so that it will work for you instead of against you.

Here is the contact information for each credit bureau:

Experian
PO BOX 9701
Allen, TX 75013
888-397-3742
www.experian.com

Trans Union
PO BOX 2002
Chester, PA 19022
800-916-8800
www.transunion.com

Equifax
PO BOX 740241
Atlanta, GA 30374
800-685-1111
www.equifax

Chapter 3
Credit
How credit reports are managed

What rights does a person have regarding their credit reports? Who governs these rights? We will tackle these questions. As you read ahead, you will understand who governs the consumer reporting agencies. You will know which acts of congress were designed to help protect you. You will learn the names of the companies that report credit. There are even companies out there you may never have heard of, that maintain information about you. We will also cover a brief history of reporting agencies. It is unsettling to know companies have eyes on us. You will learn your rights as a consumer and the avenues to keep your information accurate. With this module, you can at least keep an eye on them too.

A. History of Reporting

Let us first look at **credit bureaus**. These are companies that collect and report your credit information. We will get into whom they are further down. What I want to touch on is how it all started. Credit reporting was not what it is today. Consumer reporting agencies, before they were known as consumer reporting agencies, used to collect as much data as they could about every aspect of your life. Some would collect data that you or I would consider very private. They would then sell this information to whoever wanted it. Fortunately people did not like this and spoke up about it. The government got involved and added regulations to what can be legally reported. This regulation evolved these types of companies into the credit reporting agencies we know today. These regulations changed what type of data a company can collect and sell. These companies are not government agencies. They are publicly or privately helped corporations.

Credit reporting has evolved into a multi-billion dollar industry. Another thing to keep in mind when dealing with these companies, you are not their customer. You are a customer of their customers. Their clients are banks and lending institutions. This makes it a bit difficult to deal with them since you do not directly pay their bills. However, you do indirectly. Remember the information they have about you is their product. Since it is your information they are peddling, the acts and regulations are designed to protect you.

B. The Acts

The US government has set up various acts and laws to protect the information companies gather about you. They have also designed ways for you to verify the accuracy of the information. In the fast-paced, information changing society we live in it is important to know what rights you have and how to work with these companies. The first step is to familiarize you with the laws in place regarding the operations of these entities. They also give you insight into what rights you have with respect to the information they gather and how you can protect yourself from errors and harassment.

B.1 Federal Trade Commission Act

The *Federal Trade Commission Act* established the Federal Trade Commission in 1914. Its main functions were to promote consumer protections and eliminate anti-competitive business practices, such as monopolies. You will not have to worry about the monopoly portion of their job. The FTC can assist you with issues you may have with the consumer reporting agencies and debt collectors. They are the part of the government that enforces some of the acts we will go over.

There are three bureaus that work under the FTC. They are the Bureau of Competition, the Bureau of Economics, and the Bureau of Consumer Protection. The *Bureau of Consumer Protection* is what we will focus on here. Their main job is to protect consumers from unfair or deceptive trade practices. They enforce federal laws and rules related to consumer affairs. They work with advertising financial products, telemarketing fraud, and identity protection. This bureau is also responsible for the United States National Do Not Call Registry.

B.2 Consumer Credit Protection Act

Consumer Credit Protection Act of 1968 set restrictions on wage garnishments and led to the Truth in Lending Act of that same year. *The Truth in Lending Act* is designed to encourage the informed use of consumer credit. Terms and costs are disclosed in a standardized method as required per the act.

B.3 Fair Credit Reporting Act

The **Fair Credit Reporting Act** regulates collection, dissemination, and use of consumers' information including consumer credit information. The act was established in October 1970 and is enforced by the FTC. This act with the Fair Debt and Collection Practices act formulate the basis of consumer credit rights. This act was originally part of the Consumer Credit Protection Act.

The FCRA gives consumers the right to request the information the consumer reporting agencies have on them. This act also gives consumers the right to dispute and have the accuracy of their credit reports verified. If negative information is removed, it cannot be reinserted unless the consumer is notified in writing within five days. The FCRA also sets the retentions time of negative information.

Negative information includes lates, bankruptcies, tax liens, and judgments. The retention time for negative items is seven to ten years. The consumer reporting agencies are not the only companies that fall under the rules established by the FCRA. Companies that keep track of medical payment data, residential history, check payment history, employment history, and insurance claims, are bound by the regulations set by the FCRA. These are referred to as **nationwide specialty consumer reporting agencies**.

Information furnishers are also required to follow guidelines to be able to report to the consumer reporting agencies. An **information furnisher** is a creditor that a consumer has an agreement with, which reports to the CRAs. These can include credit card companies, mortgage lenders, auto finance institutions, or other lenders similar to these. Courts and third party companies like collection companies can also be information furnishers.

Information furnishers must provide complete and accurate information to the credit agencies. The duty to investigate the accuracy falls to them. They must explain why an account is reported in the manner it is. If the account is displayed incorrectly, they must correct it. In most cases, they have to complete these investigations in 30 days. They must inform you of negative information that has been placed or is about to be placed on your report within 30 days also. Entities that look at your report must inform you if adverse action was taken based on the information they reviewed. **Adverse action** is any reason which prevented you from obtaining the service or interest rate you were looking for. They must also identify which CRA provided the report. This is so that you can obtain a copy to review the accuracy of it.

B.4 Fair Debt Collection Practices Act

Fair Debt Collection Practices Act is an addition to the Consumer Credit Protection Act. This act establishes legal protection from abusive debt collection tactics. It also gives consumers the ability to dispute the validity of a debt. It established guidelines for debt collectors to conduct business. It also has penalties if a debt collector fails to follow the established guidelines. *Debt collectors* are organizations that collect on consumer debt. This could be a collection company or attorney who is a glorified debt collector. Attorneys collecting debts are just debt collectors.

Debt collectors can only contact you between the hours of 8 am to 9 pm, in your local time zone. If you request that they not contact you, they must comply. The only exceptions are to let you know they are not contacting you, and to inform you if they are filing a suit against you. If they tell you they are filing suit against you, they must do it. They cannot continue to contact you in a harassing manner or attempt to annoy you by repeatedly calling. They cannot contact you at your place of employment if you ask them not to. They cannot contact you directly if you have legal representation. They cannot deceive you or misrepresent the debt. In almost every instance you deal with a debt collector, they will violate the FDCPA. They just can't help themselves.

For example, they cannot say that they are law enforcement coming to arrest you if you do not pay them. They are not able to publish you to any lists showing you as a bad debtor. They cannot seek amounts that are not established by the original contract. Using abusive language is also prohibited. They cannot discuss your debt with third parties. They also cannot send potentially embarrassing mailing, like post cards, which could enable others to read about the alleged debt. Reporting false information to the credit report is also forbidden.

There are also required notifications that a debt collector has to give you. Whenever you are contacted by one, in writing or by phone, they need to inform you they are a debt collector and the purpose of contact is to collect a debt. They also must identify themselves. If you request it, they are required to give you the name and address of the original creditor, if within 30 days of the §1692g notice. A *§1692g notice* is a notification of the debt from the collector. It is required to be sent within 30 days of the initial communication between the debt collector and the consumer. Within 30 days after receiving a §1692g notice, you can (and absolutely should) request verification of the debt. The debt collector must verify it or cease collection efforts until they do verify the debt. Often this debt validation letter will be enough to scare off debt collectors as you will be more trouble than you are worth. Less than 5% of alleged debtors respond to collection letters. It just makes good business sense to focus on the easy prey that did not send a debt validation letter.

A debt validation letter is simple. It just says you demand that the account be validated before collection continues. Here is a simple example:

Date

Collection company name
Collection company address

Your name
Your address

Alleged account: 123456

Dear Collection Company,

I am writing to dispute the debt that you sent me a collection letter for (date). I received this letter within 30 days of sending this dispute letter. It is your legal responsibly to validate this alleged debt before continuing collection activities.

Sincerely,
Your name

It is important to make a copy of this letter for your records. Also, send the letter certified mail. This is legal proof that they received the letter should they deny the letter as they often do.

Verification must include the minimum amount owed and the contact information of the original creditor. After 30 days, the debt collector is not required to verify the debt although you can continue to ask for it and dispute the debt. It is important to check your mail and read carefully if you have received notification from collectors. You may miss a §1692g notice if you are not careful. If a debt collector attempts to sue you, it must be in the place where you live or signed the contract. For violations of any of the above listed restrictions and requirement, you have the right to file a suit against the collection company. The FTC also enforces these guidelines so for any violations, you can report to them.

Fair and Accurate Credit Transactions Act of 2003 amends the FCRA. It allows consumers to obtain a consumer credit report from the consumer reporting agencies for free, once every twelve months. The FTC with the consumer reporting agencies set up annualcreditreport.com and the number (877)322-8228 for obtaining that report.

The act calls for additional fraud prevention measures. With the act, you are able to add *fraud victim alert* statements and *military service statements*. These statements prevent new lines of credit from opening without contacting you first. The statement also entitles you to a copy of your credit report. The act also calls for proper secure disposal of consumer information. Credit card numbers are no longer printed on receipts due to this act being signed.

If fraud is found on the credit report and proof is submitted, the credit reporting agencies must suppress the information. The information must be blocked within four days of receiving proof. Proof would include a police report acknowledging the identity theft or a letter from the creditor verifying the account or transaction is fraudulent. This requires the credit bureaus be in contact with one another regarding identity theft issues.

B.5 Consumer Financial Protection Bureau

The *Consumer Financial Protection Bureau* is the federal agency responsible for regulation of consumer protection from financial products and services in the US. They govern banks, credit unions, securities firms, payday lenders, mortgage servicing, debt collectors, foreclosure relief, student loans, credit card companies, and any other financial related company. The bureau came into existence because of the *Dodd-Frank Wall Street Reform and Consumer Protections Act*. In July of 2011, the CFPB began operations. This bureau works with the FTC regarding the regulation of the aforementioned acts.

C. Consumer Reporting Agencies and Others

Knowing the laws that govern the reporting agencies is important, but it is equally important to know who these agencies are. We will give a brief history of each Consumer Reporting Agency and some entities that also fall under the FCRA's jurisdiction. Again, it is important to know that these are corporations and not government agencies. They have products that involve your information, but their main purpose is to make money from that information.

Credit reporting, as we know it today, is a fairly new industry. Before these companies existed, there were smaller companies that did the same thing for smaller regions. Before that, banks made decisions based on their own records. Credit and lending was more personalized. Experian, Equifax, and Trans Union expanded and purchased smaller credit bureaus and expanded their services to become what they are today.

C.1 Experian

Experian is headquartered in Dublin Ireland. Its operational headquarters are in Nottingham UK, Costa Mesa California US, and Sao Paulo Brazil. Most of what is done in the United States is run by their headquarters in Costa Mesa. They have offices in Allen, Texas for people to order and dispute their credit information. They also have a walk in office in Santa Anna, California specifically set up for disputing the credit report in person.

It is the largest of the three major credit bureaus. Experian employs roughly 17,000 people worldwide. Experian was created in 1996, when GUS Plc. acquired TRW Information Systems & Services of the United Kingdom. They then merged TRW with CCN group to create Experian. In 2006, Experian was de-merged from GUS Plc. and listed on the London Stock Exchange.
Experian works in other fields besides credit reporting. They have their hands in marketing services, decision analytics, and consumer services. The company houses information about people, businesses, motor vehicles, and insurance.

C.2 Equifax

Equifax was founded in 1899 as Retail Credit Company. It is the oldest of the three major credit bureaus. They are based out of Atlanta, Georgia. They employ over 7,000 people in 14 different countries. They used to collect information about statistics, rumors, inaccuracies, marital troubles, job history, school history, sex life, and political activities. This led to the formation of the FCRA, giving people rights about what a company can collect about them.

Equifax sells consumer credit reports and related analytical data to its business partners. They also provide commercial credit reports. They collect separate data, which generally is not included in credit reports, such as utility information also. This is considered alternative reporting data. **Alternative data** is data you do not normally find on a credit report. This includes utilities, rent, telecommunications, insurance, and electronic payments.

C.3 Trans Union

Trans Union is the third largest credit bureau in the US. If you think it sounds like a company that deals with trains, you are partially correct. Union Tank Car Company created it in 1968. It is based out of Chicago, Illinois. In 1969, they acquired the Credit Bureau of Cook County, which got them into credit reporting.

The purchase of the Credit Bureau of Cook County included almost 4 million card files in 400 seven-drawer cabinets. This led Trans Union to be the front-runner in implementing new technologies for data storage. In 1988, Tran Union had full credit reporting coverage of the United States. It operates in 32 countries worldwide.

C.4 Innovis

Some of you may receive letters from your creditors mentioning the "four" credit bureaus. **Innovis** is the fourth credit bureau. It is not as well known as the other three. It is also not as large. It has around 2,000 employees with revenue of $175 million annually. Innovis began in 1970. CBC Companies currently own it. You may see it referred to as CBCInnovis.

C.5 Alternative Data

We have mentioned alternative data. The credit reporting agencies dabble in this. Experian owns Rent Bureau, a company that stores rental history. It has rental history of over 7 million Americans. Some telecommunications companies have begun reporting to the major credit bureaus also. Trans Union recently added a product that reports alternative data. Lexis Nexis and First American CredCo are also rolling out alternative data reports.

Other companies specifically work with alternative data. **PRBC**, which stands for pay rent build credit, is a company that allows consumers to self-enroll and update their information and history with PRBC. PRBC can be considered the fifth credit-reporting agency in the US.

C.6 Chex Systems

After alternative data, we find other companies regulated by the FCRA in part. This is because their products are not necessarily credit related. **Chex Systems** is most likely the one you will see when working with banks. They are an eFunds check verification company, which also handles consumer credit reporting. Four out of five banks in the US use Chex Systems for the application process when applying for a bank account or checking account. Chex Systems' reports contain information such as: checking overdrafts, unsatisfied balances, depositing fraudulent checks, and suspicious account handling over the previous five-year period. The reporting of this type of information enables its information to be regulated by the FCRA. You can obtain a free annual Chex Systems report and dispute it as you do with the consumer reporting agencies.

C.7 Specialty Consumer Reporting Agencies

Some other companies you may deal with that are regulated by the FCRA:

Retail Equation
Central Credit
Teletrack
Medical Information Bureau
United Health Group
Milliman
Telecheck
Choice Point
Acxiom
Integrated Screening Partners
Insurance Services Office
Tenant Data Services
Lexis Nexi
Companies like these are considered specialty consumer reporting agencies. These are not required to have a central source to access their credit and data reports like the three major agencies. These are just required to give you a toll free number to request the data they have about you. Credit reports are not their main form of business, but they do collect information on other types of transactions. Depending on what you do, you may encounter one of these companies.

D. Conclusion

You are now familiar with your rights regarding consumer reporting agencies and companies that report and collect debt and other transactions. These companies track your financial wellbeing. It is imperative that you keep up with their information, at least through the free sources available. These companies will not modify their information unless you let them know it is incorrect. Even then, it can be a daunting process. When working with these companies, remember that the law requires them to report accurate information.

Do not let collection companies threaten or bully you. You have rights. If you feel any of your rights are being violated, stand up for yourself. There are ways to stop them and maybe even receive compensation if they violate the FDCPA. Collection companies almost always violate the FDCPA making it much easier to stand up for yourself.

Chapter 4
What is Credit Repair?

Credit repair is such a vague term that confuses many people about its correct definition. Some people think that credit repair is all about debt settlement or credit counseling but nothing can be further from the truth. The most correct definition of credit repair is credit correction which implies that you are repairing or cleaning your credit report. It is therefore the process of removing all negative information that can tarnish your credit report. This may also involve working with your current creditors so that they will stop reporting all negative information to credit bureaus so that you can improve your credit score which can lead to lowering your interest rates.

The best credit repair companies not only help you clean up negative items, but also help you build new credit. This new credit is important to make your credit score climb. If you engage a credit repair company, make sure they have a plan for you to add new credit lines as part of their overall strategy to improve your credit.

Hiring a credit repair company is not necessary. All of the methods we discuss can be done by you with a PC and a printer. You will need to be diligent and maintain excellent records of your communications and results.

A. How Is Credit Report Obtained

Many people find it difficult to imagine how credit report is obtained. Credit report is obtained by passing credit information to a network of financially-related institutions. For instance, when a customer files for an application for credit in a bank, the information is forwarded to a credit bureau. The credit bureau then matches the name, address as well as other distinct information of the customer with the information retained by the credit bureau in its files. As a smart consumer, it is important that you provide accurate information to your creditors so that you will not encounter any problems with the credit bureau. The problem with providing the wrong information to lenders is that the information might be credited to the wrong individual. There are several institutions that make use of the credit information and below is a brief discussion in order to understand what credit report is all about:

Credit report is used by lenders like credit card companies in order to determine the credit worthiness of a particular individual. Credit worthiness is defined as the ability of an individual to repay his or her debt. This is usually indicated by how timely the past payments were made to the lenders. In general, lenders are more confident to entertain consumers who pay their debt obligations regularly than those who don't.

Having a good credit report is very important and aside from lowering your interest rates, it is also one of the pre-qualifiers when it comes to obtaining loans from any financial institutions. Moreover, the credit report can also affect your insurance claims and may also lower your employment opportunities. Apparently, a credit report serves as your financial summary and anything negative in that report can ruin your financial reputation.

Those who also seek to get home loans will likely be subjected to investigation of their credit report. In the United States, countless of people have been denied of home loans because of having negative credit report.

Credit report may just be a piece of document but it is a very important document that gives your lenders the idea of your financial history and summary. This is the reason why it is important that you repair your negative credit report.

B. Credit History and Credit Repair

There are a number of reasons why consumers experience bad credit report. A bad credit report can be obtained due to divorce, downsizing, unemployment and extraneous medical fees stemming from medical injuries or diseases. Although these are logical reasons why people go into debts that eventually hurt their credit reports, creditors are apparently not forgiving about it.

Knowing your credit history is essential to credit repair. Credit history is compiled by credit bureaus and the data include detailed information including payment history, balances, credit limits and any overdue debts of individuals. It is important to take note that the interest rates of loans are greatly affected by the credit history thus a high credit rating equates to lower interest rates and vice versa.

Compiling such information is very crucial when it comes to determining whether a particular person is capable of making a loan and paying it. Moreover, it will also be reviewed by the lender in order to determine whether or not to approve a loan and on what terms.

The account information that is reported by your creditors is called trade lines on the credit report and this will also be used to determine the FICO or credit score. The credit score is used by creditors to determine whether a particular individual is credit worthy. Moreover, the credit score also determines the type of interest rate that you will need to pay whenever an individual makes a loan in any financial institutions.

The information contained in the credit report is then sold by different credit agencies thus an individual that has negative credit training will have a reduced likelihood of getting his or her credit application approved by a financial institution.

D. Is Credit Report Accurate

There has been a lot of discussion regarding the accuracy of credit reports. Although many industry participants claim that credit reports are accurate, there are still those who argue that disputes can still occur due to errors in credit report. Although accurate or not, it is still the right of consumers to claim disputes should they notice discrepancies on their credit report. In the next subheading, we will give a discussion on how you can file for disputes related to inaccuracy of your credit report.

E. How to File For Disputes in Credit Report Accuracy

There are some people who want to deal with their negative credit report in order to be able to make them look good to their creditors. Have you ever read or heard something to the effect:

"It is important to take note that nobody can legally remove any accurate negative information from a credit report."

This statement is a lie. Let us explain with an example.

If you have a car loan that ended in repossession. You think the amount of the loan is not correct. You dispute the debt and send in the appropriate letter. The credit reporting company cannot verify the account. They remove the account. Later you get a collection letter from the bank trying to collect the debt. You discover that the credit report had the correct amount according to the bank. Did anyone do anything illegal or unethical? No.

Most of the issues dealing with negative issues on a credit report are a matter of your ethics. We will discuss ethics later.

Consumers can ask for an investigation or file for a dispute regarding the inaccuracy or incompetency of the credit report. You can dispute all accounts negative or positive. You most likely do not want to dispute positive accounts even if you don't know what they are.

When making a dispute, it usually does not cost anything to file for one. Both the information provider and the credit reporting company are responsible for correcting inaccurate information in your credit report. The information provider is any individual, entity or organization that provides information to the credit reporting company. Below are some examples on how to file for dispute of inaccurate credit report.

o It is important that you inform the credit reporting company the information that you claim is inaccurate through a written letter. It is also crucial that you include copies of documents that will support your claim, if you have them. Moreover, the letter should also clearly indicate each item in the report that you dispute and the reasons why you dispute such information.

o Once the credit reporting company receives your letter of dispute, they need to investigate your claim within 30 days unless there is any suspicion on the validity of your dispute. They will also send your relevant data including your letter to the ones who provided them with your credit information. If the investigation revealed that there is indeed an inaccuracy in the credit report, the information provider will usually be the one to notify credit reporting companies in order to correct your file.

o After the investigation, it is important that the credit reporting company give you [the consumer] the results in writing. Moreover, a free copy of the new report should also be provided. It is also important that you ask the credit reporting company to send notices of the correction to anyone who got your inaccurate credit report within the last six months. For instance, you can require a corrected copy be sent to your employer especially if your employer has asked you for your credit report upon employment.

F. How to Deal with Accurate Negative Information

Take note that a credit reporting company can report accurate negative information for seven years while it can report bankruptcy information for 10 years. Negative information will likely not go away for at least 7 years on its own. Moreover, information regarding unpaid judgment can be reported for seven years maximum until the statute of limitations eventually runs out. This seven year reporting usually starts from the date the accurate negative information took place.

G. Steps on How to Do Credit Repair

There is a whole bunch of information online that discuss about how to do credit repair. Most of this information is either generic or junk. If you do no heed our advice in this book, make sure the advice you follow gets results and is within your sense of ethics. Basically, credit repair can be done by yourself and below are the tips on how you can do credit repair by yourself before opting to hire credit repair companies.

- Get a copy of your credit report from credit reporting companies. It is important to take note that credit reports are free and you can obtain them from any credit reporting companies of your choice.

- If you take note of some inaccuracies in the credit report, you can file for a dispute with the creditors that have sent your information to credit reporting companies. Remember that you can only dispute information that you strongly believe is inaccurate.

- Contact each of your creditors and ask if they are willing to give you a repayment plan that you can afford. This will also assure your creditors your intent to repay the debt that you owe them.

- You can also contact your creditors and ask them if they can reduce the interest rates applied on your credit card debt, if any. Some creditors may be willing to give you this ease. Once you are given a reduction in your interest, you can use it to pay for your debt faster.

- Account all bills within a year. The bills include your household utility, mortgage, home insurance and retirement contributions. Make sure that you create a budget that will help you spend only what you need. The most important thing in credit repair is for you to reduce your debts to improve your credit report.

These are some tips on how you can solve your negative credit report. Doing credit repair on your own can be a lengthy procedure but if you persevere, then you will be able to solve your negative credit report so that you will have better financial reputation.

H. Credit Repair Companies

Although the ideal way to repair your credit is to let time work to heal your bad credit score or to talk with your creditors by yourself, these particular methods are somewhat impractical. Not too many people have the liberty to wait for seven or ten years so that their credit report will automatically be repaired nor do they have a lot of time to talk to each of their creditors to ask for new repayment options. One of the solutions is to hire credit repair companies.

Credit repair companies can help you repair your negative credit report. However, not too many people are too trusting about hiring such companies. Unfortunately, there are many people who got victimized by fly-by-night credit repair companies. Although this may be the case, it is important to take note that there are many legitimate credit repair companies that you can seek help to improve your credit report. Below are some of the reasons why it is so essential that you hire a credit repair company.

- o Expertise. A legitimate and professional credit repair company can help you immensely because they are familiar with laws governing credit industry. Seeking the expertise of credit repair companies will help you understand what you need to do to stop hurting your credit rating.

- o Prevention of Identity Theft. One of the reasons why there are some people who have negative credit report is identity theft. Take note that when erroneous information is provided to the lender, this information will be sent to the credit bureau which will be matched to existing names within the files of the bureau. Should credit disputes arise due to identity theft, you can hire credit repair companies to help you clear up your identity. Protecting yourself against identity theft can be downright challenging but hiring a professional credit repair company will help you see the results faster.

- Corrects Errors On Credit Reports. More than 79% of credit reports in United States contain erroneous information and by hiring a credit repair company, they will be able to help you fix your credit report immediately.

- Worry-Free Solution to Your Credit Problems. Whenever you receive a negative credit report, it often causes you too much stress thinking about how to solve your demise. However, hiring a credit repair company saves you all the trouble of worrying on what might happen to you. You do not need to feel frustrated when it comes to dealing with credit repair because a professional credit repair company will be the one to provide the solution for you. Since credit repair companies do not have emotional attachments to any cases that they handle, they can deal with the situation effectively.

- They Make The Process Shorter. Credit collecting agencies and creditors know a lot of loopholes to make credit repair a lengthy procedure. Since credit repair companies know the ins and outs of the credit industry, they can make the lengthy process of credit repair shorter.

Although there are many people who are apprehensive about hiring credit repair companies, they are still indispensable among those who suffer from negative credit reports. Thus if you want help in fixing your credit report, you should hire legitimate and professional credit repair company near you.

I. What to Do Before Hiring A Credit Repair Company

In the US, there are thousands of consumers who were taken by fraudulent credit repair companies. Although the Federal Trade Commission (FTC) serves as the watchdog against scammers posing as legitimate credit repair companies, they can only do so much to catch these unscrupulous individuals. As a result, tens of thousands of consumers have already lost their money because they hired the wrong people.

This section does not mean to scare you nor discourage you from hiring credit repair companies. It is important to take note that there are still many credit report companies that provide legitimate services and that they have been around in the industry for quite a long time. Thus as a consumer, it is important that you know how to find the right credit repair company. Below are some tips on what you need to do when it comes to looking for legitimate credit repair companies.

- Check the ECRA and see if the credit repair company is a member with good standing. The ECRA stands for Ethical Credit Repair Alliance and it is an organization that regulates credit repair companies. Credit report companies that are members of ECRA needs to abide by the Code of Professional Ethics and the Federal Law. Members who have violated the rules of the organization are subject to expulsion from the organization.

- Check whether a credit repair company has unresolved and open disputes. Make sure that the credit repair company that you wish to hire has no unresolved or open disputes. Credit repair companies that do give the impression that they are incompetent thus they might not be able to deliver your expected results.

J. How to Seek Help If You Are Victimized By Illegal Credit Repair Company

There are some credit repair companies that lie about what they can do to improve your credit report. In reality, the US credit industry is flooded by crooked credit report companies which prey on unsuspecting individuals who are desperate when it comes to looking for solutions to their problems. For this reason, the Credit Repair Organization Act (CROA) was made to protect consumers against unscrupulous credit repair companies. This act was enforced by the Federal Trade Commission. The CROA requires all credit repair companies to explain to their clients the following:

- The legal rights of clients written in contract which also includes details of the services that they will perform.
- The three-day right of clients to cancel without any charges
- The time duration on how long credit repair will be enacted
- The total cost of the credit repair
- Guarantees, if any
- The CROA can also protect you – the consumers – should the credit repair companies not deliver their promises. As a consumer, you have several options as follows:
- Sue the credit repair company for the actual losses
- Join people in a class action lawsuit so that if you win, the credit repair company will be the one to shoulder the attorney's fee.

Aside from the Credit Repair Organization Act, there are also some other ways for consumers to seek help if they become victims of unscrupulous credit repair companies. In fact, there are many ways on reporting credit repair fraud. Below are some of the options that you have to report a credit repair fraud.

J.1 State Attorney General

There are many states that have laws that regulate credit repair companies and if you happen to encounter problems with them, then you can report credit repair fraud directly to the local consumer affairs office or directly to the state attorney general. This way, you will be able to see results as soon as you make the complaints.

J.2 Free Trade Commission

The Free Trade Commission is also a great avenue for you to file your complaints against credit repair fraud. However, it is important to take note that you can only file the complaints at FTC but they do not have the capability to resolve individual credit disputes. What it can do is to take action against the erring credit repair company.

K. Alternatives to Credit Repair

Although one of the best solutions to repair your credit report is to hire a credit repair company, there are still ways for you to improve your credit report by taking alternative credit repair strategies. There are ways for you to seek legitimate help even if you have a negative credit report.

One of the most effective methods in repairing your negative credit report is to seek a credit counselor. There are many non-profit organizations that are aimed to work with individuals who need help with their negative credit score. However, it is important to take note that some credit counseling organizations do not offer their services free so you must know first whether they require payment or not before seeking them out.

Credit repair is very important because it will help you get a good credit standing with your creditors. Hopefully this section has covered everything that you need to know about credit report and credit repair.

Chapter 6
Getting To Know Credit Repair Scams

Are you one of the many people who have problems with your bad credit report? If yes, then you must have already contemplated seeking the help of a credit repair company (CRO). However, with all the news about credit repair scams, do you think that you should trust CROs? The answer is still yes.

Although there are a number of consumers who have been victimized by credit card scams, it is not good to assume that all credit repair companies are bad. There are many credit repair companies that are still legitimate and are honest in providing services to their clients. Although it cannot be helped that there are really credit repair companies that work in a fly-by-night operation, it is important that you know how to determine whether a particular credit repair company is legitimate or not.

The general rule when it comes to determining whether a particular company can deliver is that they offer guarantees to all of their clients when it comes to improving their bad credit report. Apparently, most of these companies easily vanish with your money thus you may end up in a deeper debt than you currently have. Unfortunately, those who are struggling with rebuilding their bad credit report are often the ones who are victimized by scheming credit repair companies.

A. What Are Credit Repair Companies

Credit repair companies offer services that will help you remove the bad information on your credit report. Unlike credit counselors, these companies do not offer guidance on how you can manage your finances to improve your bad credit rating. Basically, credit repair companies do entirely different processes compared with credit counselors when it comes to their services. Below are the usual steps credit repair companies follow in order to remove the negative information on your credit report:

- The credit repair companies will ask you to send then copies of your credit reports from different credit reporting agencies such as Equifax, TransUnion and Experian. Take note that the previous chapter tells you how you can get your credit report for free by simply communicating with these agencies.

- Once you send the copies of the credit report, the credit repair company will then analyze it and will suggest items on the report that you should dispute. For this particular step, it is crucial that you provide the necessary copies of your financial statements which will be used as evidence for dispute.

- When both you and the credit repair company have agreed about the items in question, the credit repair company will then contact the credit report organizations to challenge them about the items listed on your credit report.

Credit repair companies are legitimate businesses and they aim to help people especially those who believe that their negative credit information is caused by inaccuracies and lapses by the credit reporting agencies. They simply act as mediators to confirm and correct any discrepancies on the negative credit report.

B. How to Avoid Becoming a Victim of Credit Repair Scam

Hiring a shady credit repair company means that you are digging your own grave. Although it has been noted that not all credit repair companies are shady, it is still important to know the warning signs of shady credit repair companies. Below are the tell-tale signs that a particular credit repair company is just scamming you.

Credit repair companies that scam other people offer too good to be true results. Credit repair is a difficult process because there are many things that need to be considered.

- They promise to clean up your bad credit report even before knowing your real situation. All legitimate credit repair companies need to know your real situation first before they provide solutions or recommend other options for you. However, shady credit repair companies will skip all necessary investigations and will immediately offer unnecessary solutions to your problems even before knowing what the real score is and what the real problem is.

- Questionable credit repair companies do not tell you about your rights and the options that you can do by yourself. There are some options that you can do wherein you do not have to spend to repair your credit. You can contact credit reporting agencies directly or seek help from credit counselors but since shady credit repair companies are after your money, they do not tell you what you need to do because their goal is to get your money from the beginning.

- Shady credit repair companies suggest that you create a new credit identity by applying for a new Employer Identification Number. Moreover, they also do not want to use your Social Security number when creating a new credit identity. Remember, your goal is to have better credit, not to be in prison.

These are the tell-tale signs that the credit repair companies are shady and are just after your money. You have to take note that legitimate credit repair companies are transparent and that they are after helping you fix your bad credit report (if they can help it) rather than get your money.

C. Important Things to Consider When Hiring Credit Repair Companies

When hiring credit repair companies, there are some things that you need to do. One of the most important things is to have the credit repair company make a contract of the services that they provide. Creating a contract serves as your protection against questionable schemes of the credit repair company that you will hire. Moreover, the contract will also serve as your guide on what credit repair companies are capable of doing. The contract needs to specify the following things:

- The payment terms of the services should be itemized in the contract. Any hidden charges should also be indicated.

- It is important for the contract to list a detailed description of the services that the credit repair company needs to perform.

- A contract should also be bounded by time thus it is important that it should indicate how long it should take for them [credit repair company] to achieve the results.

- Do they offer any guarantees? It is important that the contract should indicate guarantees to clients especially if they cannot provide a solution to the bad credit information.

- It is also very important for the contract to indicate the name of the company, its business address and important contact information. All of the information should be legitimate.

To make the contract binding, make sure that both you and the representative from the credit repair company sign the contract. That way, you can actually take legal actions if the credit repair company fails to deliver their promises. On the other hand, a contract is also another way of telling whether a particular credit repair agency is shady or legitimate. Shady credit repair agencies cannot be bothered or they make excuses whenever their clients ask them to make a contract.

D. The Truth about Removing Negative Credit Information

Although the process of removing the negative information is ideally an easy task, the reality is far from simple. You have to understand that it is difficult to remove accurate negative information from your credit report. This process can take months. There is no way to tell how long the credit repair process will take.

E. Different Kinds of Credit Repair Scams

There are different kinds of credit repair scams and, unfortunately, there are many people who are not aware that they are already being scammed even if they are already staring at it. It is therefore important that you have knowledge about credit repair scams. Below are some of the scams that are masked as work by shady credit repair companies.

E.1 The File Segregation Scheme

How many times have you heard about credit repair companies promising their clients new credit identities? A new credit identity is defined as having a fresh start of credit history. Moreover, if you are one of the many people who have filed for bankruptcy, then shady credit repair companies will tell you that you will not be able to get credit for 10 years thus to solve your problem, they usually hide your credit information by giving you a new credit identity. The creation of new credit identity is called file segregation which is really illegal.

It will seem as a good thing that will help you get a clean slate on your credit report but the truth is that it is just a scam. There is no such thing as a new credit identity. All individuals need to have only one credit identity and if it is tarnished by having bad credit report, then there is nothing that you can do to clean it except traditional credit repair to work on diminishing your debts or reviewing whether there are some discrepancies on your credit report that you can dispute.

E.2 Getting a New Social Security Number

Some shady credit repair companies recommend their clients get new Social Security numbers. In fact, most of these companies sell Social Security numbers illegally. Most of the Social Security number that shady credit repair companies sell are obtained from children or those who have yet to have their own credit information – or basically from minors. Of course, using a number to apply for credit will not be reflected on your original credit report information but if you were found out, then you could land in prison. Take note that no one is allowed to own multiple Social Security numbers because it is clear that you are committing identity theft by doing so.

E.3 Applying For a New EIN

The Employer Identification Number (EIN) is a legitimate number that you get from the Internal Revenue Services (IRS) and it is used by businesses to report financial information to IRS as well as to the Social Security Administration. In most cases, some shady credit repair companies will ask you to apply for a new EIN to use in place of your current Social Security number. This is another good way to end up in prison.

F. How Credit Repair Companies Pitch In Their Scams

Although many people are aware that credit repair scams exist, there are still those who easily get victimized even if there is much information telling consumers on how to avoid unscrupulous credit repair companies. Apparently, shady credit repair companies are good at deceiving unsuspecting consumers. Below are the false claims that credit repair companies tell their clients to trick them to getting their services:

- o People who file for bankruptcy will not be able to get credit for 10 years. It is crucial to take note that people who have filed for bankruptcy can still get credit. Different creditors have their own criteria for granting credit and the negative credit report can easily be solved if you take on a new debt settlement or repayment plan with your creditors.

- The credit repair company is affiliated with the federal government. It is important to take note that the government does not support or work together with credit repair companies.

- Creating new credit identity is legal and a lot of people have been doing it. In reality, a lot of people who resort to credit identity end up going to jail as it equates to identity theft and fraud.

H. How the Credit Repair Organization Act Can Help You

Because there is an increased incidence of people being victimized by shady credit repair companies, the Credit Repair Organization Act (CROA) was implemented as a law in 1996. This act helps protect the public from deceptive advertising as well as bad business practices of credit repair organizations.

Under this act, all legitimate credit repair organizations are required to submit a copy of the Consumer Credit File Rights under State and Federal Law to their clients before signing a contract. This is a copy that looks like a waiver wherein consumers are informed about their rights when it comes to hiring credit repair companies. The copy should be duly signed and dated to make sure that you understand the things stipulated in the consumer credit files rights. For you to understand further, the Consumer Credit File Rights under State and Federal Law states the following:

- You have the right to take legal action against a credit repair organization that has violated the CROA.

- You have the right to terminate and cancel the contract with the credit repair company for any reasons as long as termination of contract occurs within three (3) business days from the date that you signed the contract.

- Credit bureaus need to follow procedures to make sure that the information they report is always correct. Should mistakes arise; consumers can notify the credit bureau in writing. Reinvestigation needs to be done to modify and correct the inaccurate credit information. Correction of credit information is free.

- o The Federal Trade Commission (FTC) regulates all credit repair organization and consumers have the right to know the legitimacy of credit Repair Company by contacting the Public Reference Branch of the Federal Trade Commission in Washington D.C.

The CROA is created in order to protect consumers from unscrupulous credit repair companies. Fortunately, CROA can hound credit repair companies for the inconveniences that they have caused you. They are liable for the damages that you have suffered as well as the amount that you paid them. Moreover, if they are proven guilty, they are also liable for the attorney's fee. Thus if you think that you have been duped by a bad credit repair company, you should contact FTC immediately and file a complaint. Remember that if you just go along with the plans of the shady credit repair company, you are also committing felony. It is crucial that you stop the cycle of scam by sending your complaints to FTC. You can reach them at 1-877-FTC-HELP or you can go to their website at www.ftc.gov to sue erring credit repair companies. Not only are you helping yourself achieve personal justice but you are also helping the many victims of shady credit repair companies.

Aside from reporting to the Free Trade Commission (FTC), there are some alternatives when it comes to seeking help against shady credit report companies. In many states, laws have been implemented to regulate credit repair companies. If you encounter problems, you can report it to the local consumer affairs office or directly to the state Attorney General so that the necessary actions are taken. The Attorney General can give you advice on how to resolve your problems. Fortunately, you can get the Attorney General's address in your area by visiting www.naag.org.

Another way for you to seek help is to tap the Consumer Action which is a non-profit organization that offers consumer advice and referrals to the agencies that handle complaints against shady credit repair agencies. The website of Consumer Action is www.consumer-action.org.

I. Protecting Yourself against Shady Credit Repair Companies

In the previous sections, this chapter discussed the different types of credit repair scams that consumers are highly at risk of. Moreover, the section also discussed about how to seek help in case you have been victimized by shady credit repair companies as well as how to know to tell whether a particular company is shady or not. Protecting yourself against shady credit repair companies is very important so that you will not have to suffer even more. Having a negative credit rating is already bad as it is, but being victimized by shady credit repair companies make the situation worse.

If you are unsure about the legitimacy of a particular credit repair company, then you can always contact the Better Business Bureau and check whether a particular credit repair company is listed or not. Hire companies that have good records on the Better Business Bureau as they are credible.

On the other hand, remember that there are no guarantees to credit repairs so if a particular company offers guarantee (except the money back guarantee), then you should view it with a skeptical eye.

You might not be a wise spender before but this does not mean that you shouldn't be a wise consumer when it comes to picking up credit repair companies that will help you solve your problems. It is important that you be careful whenever responding to credit repair ads and make sure that you report fraudulent repair credit repair companies immediately. Take note that it is hard to put a stop to credit repair scam unless victims complain about them.

Chapter 7
Coping With Debt

An average American household has about $15,112 on credit card debt alone according to the Federal Reserve Statistics. Aside from credit card debt, people also incur different kinds of debts from their mortgage to student loans. The same 2013 statistics released by the Federal Reserve indicated that the American consumers owe a total of $11.08 trillion in debt and the number of debt will likely increase to 10.9% the following year due to the slightly poor performance of the country.

Although debt is unnecessary, there are still so many people who suffer from it. Before understanding what needs to be done in order to cope up from debt, it is important to understand the types of debts and the psychology of debt and why people are buried up to their necks paying debts.

A. Types of Debts

There are two types of debts which include secured and unsecured debts. The former are debts that are tied to assets like homes for mortgage loans and cars for car loans. What happens when you stop making payments on your secured debts is that the lenders are likely to repossess your assets. On the other hand, unsecured debts are not usually tied to your assets and they include most of your credit card debt, medical care debts as well as signature loans. Knowing about the two types of debts is very important because it allows you to understand what will happen should you fail to pay a particular type of debt.

Moreover, this will also allow you to know the necessary steps that you should take in order to protect your credit rating. For instance, if you make a car loan and you cannot pay for it completely, then the creditor has the right to repossess your car during default. If you notice that your car loan is in danger of being defaulted, then you can sell the car yourself and pay your debt. That way, you will be able to avoid the cost of repossession and also getting negative information on your credit report.

B. Why People Incur Debts

There are many reasons why people incur debts. One of the reasons is that many people go into deficit spending. This occurs when you spend more than what you earn in a given time. If you constantly do deficit spending, what happens is that your accumulated deficit becomes debt which then becomes a financial obligation that you need to pay.

Another reason why people go into debt is due to unforeseeable events. There are some events wherein people will be forced to borrow money to fund for emergency situations. Such situations include paying exorbitant medical fees, a loss of job or damage to one's properties. Although these circumstances may rarely occur, it is still important to take note that once they happen, you will be expected to spend a lot of if you have not prepared for it.

Another reason why people end up going into debt is because of their lifestyle. There are many people who like to buy things that they do not need in order to feel happy. This is called retail therapy. More often than not, people who do retail therapy feel fleeting happiness but end up feeling guilty after realizing that they have incurred a lot of debts during the day.

Lastly, a lot of people go into debt because of self-denial and ignorance. Currently, credit card debt is very high and this is one of the debts that consumers find difficult to settle. Although credit cards are convenient, those who do not know how credit card interest rates work or know the implication of making minimum payments often escalate their debt problems. Consumer debt is very serious and almost all elegible American wage-earners incur a lot of debts that they can manage. For this reason it is important to know methods on how to ease credit card debts.

C. What Happens If You Owe Debt That You Cannot Pay?

There are times when a borrower is unable to pay debts that they owe. Although you are somewhat likely to get sued by the creditor for not honoring the contract, it is against the law for the creditor to do anything such as contacting your employer or family members and informing them about the debts before getting any court judgment. Moreover, they [creditors] are also not allowed to threaten you with jail nor harass your family about your debts. Even if you owe a lot of debts, you are still protected by the law. The main law that covers how collectors can interact with you is the FDCPA. For more information on the FDCPA, visit Boiler's website at notlegaladvice.org

D. Strategies on How to Cope From Debts

Although debtors are protected by the law, this does not mean that you have to be lax when it comes to settling your debts. If not addressed and settled soon, you might end up having a lot of problems. Moreover, you will also end up tarnishing your credit rating if you do not settle your debts. When it comes to easing debts, some people do credit repair but, aside from credit repair, there are still a lot of things that can be done in order to cope from debts. Below are strategies that will help you cope from your debts.

D.1 Develop a budget

The reason why most people end up incurring a lot of debts is that they cannot control their finances and they are not realistic enough when it comes to spending their money. The best solution to the problem is to first know how to develop a budget. When developing a budget, make sure that you list your fixed expenses such as mortgage payments and insurances. Listing variable expenses such as groceries and clothing is also important. By creating a budget, you will be able to determine your spending habits, thus you will be able to find out whether you are spending too much on things that you do not really need. It is important to take note that when developing a budget you need to focus more on providing for your needs and not your wants.

D.2 Contact Your Creditors

Some people do not know that they can contact their creditors to give them new repayment plans. Most creditors will be more than willing to listen to your request in modifying the payment plan to a more manageable level. In most cases, your creditors will be happy that you are still thinking about paying them. The thing about contacting your creditors and letting them know about your financial demise is for them to give you ease of payment as well as to prevent them from turning over your debts to debt collectors.

On the other hand, if your creditors have already handed your debts to debt collectors, you have to take note that debt collectors are unforgiving about unsettled debts. Many people are fearful of debt collectors as there have been many stories regarding them [debt collectors] harassing people.

Remember that debt collectors may have the right to get payment from you but you still retain the right to be able to protect yourself against harassments from debt collectors.

D.3 Get Debt Relief Services

People who struggle with their debts and cannot work a repayment plan with their creditors may get debt relief services. This particular type of service is similar to credit counseling as you get advice on how you should deal with your mounting bills.

There are many companies that offer debt relief services but before you do business with them, it is crucial that you check with the state Attorney General or with your local consumer protection agency to determine whether a particular debt relief services firm is legitimate and licensed. Moreover, it is also important that you find out about the type of services that they provide, the cost and how long the will be able to deliver the results that you want.

Be cautious as most of debt relief services are a glorified collection agency at best. Often debt relief services collect money from you for months before disbursing the money you have ear marked for your debts.

D.4 Credit Counseling

One of the most popular options when it comes to coping up with debts is to seek a reliable credit counseling organization that can advise you on how you can manage your finances and develop a budget by offering educational workshops. The best thing about seeking a credit counseling organization is that credit counselors can help you create a personalized plan in order to solve your money problems. The counseling session may last for an hour and can be done in a classroom setting or a one-on-one session.

You do not need to pay for the services of credit counselors as there are reputable credit counseling organizations that provide their services for free.

D.5 Debt Management Plans

Another option among people who have problems with debts is to seek debt management plans. Most credit counseling agencies will recommend this particular service to people who are suffering from debts. It is important to take note that debt management plans are not for everyone thus it is important to seek the help of a credit counselor to assess your financial situation to ensure that you are capable of doing this particular strategy or not.

In a debt management plan, you need to deposit money every month with the credit counseling organization. The money that you deposited to the credit counseling organization will be used to pay for any unsecured debts that you may have depending on the payment schedule set by the counselor. With the intervention of the credit counseling organizations, there is a possibility that you can lower your interest rates as well as waive your other fees. A successful debt management plan relies on your ability to make regular and timely payments. It might take you more than a year or more to completely pay off your debt depending on the amount that you owe your creditors.

To safeguard yourself from this particular option, it is important that you check with your creditors to be sure that they offer concessions with the credit counseling company that you have sought help with.

Again, like debt relief services, debt management is rife with deceit and fraud; often taking your hard earned cash without paying your creditors.

D.6 Debt Settlement Programs

Debt settlement program is similar with debt management plan because it requires you to set aside an amount of money every month to pay off debt. However, the difference between the two is that the debt settlement program is offered by for-profit companies and it usually involves companies to negotiate with the creditors to give you a settlement program to resolve your debt.

While this particular option sounds great, it is important to take note that this particular program comes with risks. Below are the risks involved if you opt for this particular program to cope up with your debts:

- o The debt management program requires you to deposit your money in a special savings account for 36 months or more until your debts are settled. Because of the longer time duration needed to make regular deposits, some people have problems withstanding the long payments and they end up dropping off the program sooner than expected.

Thus, before signing for this particular program, it is important that you review your budget and financial stats first before you start this program.

- There are some creditors who are not obligated to negotiate a settlement with you. There is also a possibility that the debt settlement company will not be able to settle your debts even though you are stringent in setting aside money as required by the program.

- If they can negotiate with the creditors, some debt settlement companies also negotiate for smaller debts first thus you end up with higher interests and fees instead.

- The debt settlement program requires you to stop sending your payments directly to the creditors so it will definitely have a negative impact on your credit report. Since the main idea of a debt settlement program is for you to save enough money to pay off all your debts, you end up accruing late fees or penalties which can further your financial demise. If your debt settlement company does not work together with your creditors, then your creditors will rely on debt collectors which might put you in a lot of inconvenience.

Although there are some risks of debt settlement programs, it still remains as one of the most popular options for people. If you are one of the many people who are looking into debt settlement to pay off your debts, it is important to avoid debt settlement scams to protect yourself from making your financial situation even worse. Below are some things that you need to do before hiring a debt settlement company.

- The Federal Trade Commission highly discourages companies that offer debt settlement programs via the phone. As much as possible, it is important for consumers with debts to visit the office of debt settlement companies so that they will be able to get the right information that they need in order to understand the program fully.

- When you hire a debt settlement agency, you need to put your money in a dedicated bank account. It is important to take note that even if the debt settlement agency is considered as an independent third party, they do not have full control over your account. Since the funds are yours, you are entitled to any interests accrued by your funds. And since the fund is yours, you can withdraw it anytime you want without paying for any penalty fees.

o   Before you get the services from a debt settlement agency, it is important that you
    know about the disclosure requirements. The disclosure requirements include the price
    and terms of the services that they provide, the duration of the results and guarantees if
    any.

E. What To Avoid When Hiring Debt Settlement Companies

It is important to practice caution when it comes to hiring debt settlement companies. Whether you are hiring credit counseling, debt settlement agencies and other similar organizations for that matter, it is important that you understand what to avoid when hiring them. Below are some of the things that will serve as your tell-tale sign that you debt settlement company might be scamming you:

- They charge fees before they settle your debts
- They pressure you to make voluntary contributions
- They suggest a new government program so that you can bail out personal credit card debt
- They can guarantee to relieve your debts no matter what
- They enroll you in a debt relief program without even reviewing your financial situation
- Discourage you from communicating with your creditors without giving you the proper explanation
- Enroll you in a debt relief program without teaching you important skills like budgeting and handling your money.

F. Debt Consolidation

It may be possible to reduce the cost of your credit by means of consolidating your debt. This can be achieved by getting a second mortgage or an equity line of credit. This particular debt easing strategy is great if you have secured debts such as a home mortgage. You can extend paying off your debts if you apply for debt consolidation but the problem is that you need to put up your assets as collateral and if you cannot make any payments, then you end up losing your assets. Moreover, debt consolidation also comes with costs and aside from the interest that you need to pay, you also need to pay an amount that is equal to one percent of the amount that you borrow.

G. Filing for Bankruptcy

Filing for bankruptcy is another option that many people have to ease themselves from their debts. People who file for bankruptcy get a court order that indicates that they do not have to repay certain debts. Although this will relieve you from certain financial obligations, the bankruptcy information stays in your credit report for 10 years thus making it difficult for you to get credit, get mortgage or even buy a life insurance. Moreover, some employers also are partial against employees who have bankruptcy records. This option should be your last resort.

There are two types of personal bankruptcy that you can file and these include Chapter 7 and Chapter 13. Both types of personal bankruptcy can be filed in the federal bankruptcy court. Below is a brief discussion between the differences of the two types of personal bankruptcy.

Chapter 13 allows people who have a steady stream of income to keep certain assets such as their homes or cars. This particular bankruptcy allows the debtor to undergo a repayment plan to pay off their debts between three and five years. After making the payments, the debtor is relieved from his or her debts.

Chapter 7 is the most common type of personal bankruptcy filed by many people. It involves the liquidation of all assets and sold by court-appointed officials or turned over to creditors to pay for the debts.

Both types of bankruptcy help rid you of unsecured debts and prevent foreclosure. However, it is important take note that child support, taxes, student loans and alimony are not covered by personal bankruptcy and you still need to pay for them even if you have already filed for bankruptcy at court.

On the other hand, people who have bankruptcy also need to get credit counseling from government-approved organizations. This is to ensure that you will be able to correct your financial situation after filing for bankruptcy.

These are examples of strategies that you can adapt in order to ease yourself from your debts. When deciding which option is good for you, it is important that you consider your financial status as well as your goal. In any case, seeking help from a credit counseling organization will also help you prevent making mistakes that can make your financial situation even messier.

Chapter 8
DIY Tips for Repairing Your Credit Score

Many people incur debts and one of the most common debts consumers make are credit card debts. The average credit card debt of US households is $15,799 and there are an astounding 15% of American families whose debts exceed 40% of their household income. Having said this, most people live today with insurmountable debts that they cannot handle.

Having debts and not being able to pay for them often leads to having a bad credit score. A bad credit score often reflects the unstable financial situation of consumers. Moreover, a bad credit score often leads to people not being able to get credit unless they do something about it.

A. Understanding Credit Score

In the previous chapters, credit score is defined as the numerical expression that is based on an individual's credit files. A credit score is used to gauge the credit worthiness of a consumer thus having a good credit score means that a consumer is capable of paying off their debts.

Primarily, a credit score is based on the credit report information submitted to credit bureaus. The credit score is used by banks, lenders and other financial institutions to assess the risk posed by the lender. In fact, this is one of the parameters financial institutions look for when it comes to determining whether they should grant loans or credit applications to consumers.

If you are suffering from a bad credit score, it is important that you deal with the situation so that you will be able to look good to your future creditors. There are many people who think that there is nothing that they can do in order to improve their credit score. In reality, your poor credit score can always be improved.

B. Don't Borrow Money to Get Out of Debt

This may seem like common sense, but you cannot borrow money to get out of debt. This is not common sense as people try to do this every hour of everyday. If you learn anything from this book remember this truism: **You cannot borrow your way out of debt**. This plan will never work for you (and it will never work for our government).

For example, if you owe $20,000 on credit cards and open a HELOC with your house as collateral. You pay off the credit cards with the new house loan. You still owe the money. What you may have done is lowered your interest rate. If you take out a new loan to get a better interest rate that is a perfectly good reason to lower your interest rate. It will take some self-control not to run up your credit cards again and be in worse shape than you are in now.

C. DIY Repair of Credit Score

There are many ways you can improve a bad credit report. Although you can take on recommended credit repair programs (see authors credits for this book), you can still do DIY repair on your bad credit score. There are many advantages of doing DIY repair on your bad credit score and below is a brief discussion on why you should do DIY credit score repair:

- It helps instill financial discipline. The most important advantage of doing DIY credit repair is that it helps develop financial discipline. Most people who are buried up to their necks with debt often amass a lot of deficits because of their inability to control their spending. By doing DIY credit score repair, you will be able to value your finances more and develop a discipline to only spend your money where it is needed.

- It helps you understand your financial status. Some people incur debts because they do not understand their financial status. Thus doing DIY credit score repair will help you realize your financial capabilities.

- It is cheaper... or is it? Being in debt and hiring a credit repair company or credit counselors to help you with your credit problems may cost you more, thus doing DIY credit repair will help you improve your bad credit score without the need for you to break your bank. Are you really going to keep after the credit reporting agencies and keep immaculate records, or do you need some help? When you consider the cost of credit repair, weigh the cost against the cost of having bad credit. It will likely be cheaper to hire a good credit repair company than to do nothing. It will also reduce your stress to know your credit is on the mend.

- You avoid potential scams from unscrupulous credit repair companies. The problem about seeking credit repair companies or debt settlement firms is that you are at risk of being involved in scams. However, doing DIY credit repair prevents you from getting involved in scams because you will be the one doing everything to improve your credit report.

o You will learn the fundamentals of credit. The best thing about repairing your credit is that you get a free lesson on the fundamentals of credit. Through your research, you will learn what makes a credit score good or bad. Moreover, you will develop the necessary disciplines that will help you improve and maintain your credit score in the future.

o You have control over the entire process. When you handle your own credit repair, you will be able to know what is going on with the entire process. You also understand the credit repair process more if you do DIY credit repair than hiring a credit repair company. If you are a person that has no interest in the process, it might serve you better to hire a credit repair company.

D. How to Improve Your Credit Score

When you do credit repair, it is important to take note that it takes a lot of discipline to be able to do DIY repair. It also takes a lot of time to fix your credit score and that there are no quick fixes available that will help you improve your credit. Below are some important tips to get you started with your DIY credit score repair.

1. The first thing that you need to do is to check your credit report. It is crucial to get all three credit reports from Equifax, Experian and TransUnion so that you can compare for discrepancies in the credit reports generated by the three agencies. All legitimate credit repair always begins with looking at your credit reports. If you do not have your credit report yet, you can always get a free copy from credit reporting bureaus. Once you have your credit report, you can check it for any errors. There are many errors on most people's credit reports. Check whether your credit report does not have any posted late payments. You can also use receipts to compare that the information on your credit report is correct. If there are errors, then you can use it as grounds for dispute. If there are no errors, then you have to develop strategies in order to improve your bad credit score.

2. Set up regular payment reminders. In order to improve your credit score, it is important that you make regular credit payments to your creditors. There are some creditors that offer payment reminders so you can avail of this service to always remind you to make

your payments before the due date. On the other hand, you can also enroll in automatic payments so that your creditors can debit the payment from your bank account.

3. Reduce your debts. Reducing your debt requires a lot of discipline on your part. This means that you have to prioritize paying off your debts and avoiding situations where you are sure to incur more debts than you can handle. For instance, if you love to use your credit card, then the most important thing that you should do is to give up using the card. It might be a drastic move but doing this will prevent you from using your credit card further. When reducing your debt, it is important that you determine how much you owe from each of your creditors and make plans accordingly. Budget your money wisely and for the first two years, dedicate your most of your time in paying off and reducing your debts.

4. Improve your credit score by dealing with the five factors used to calculate your FICO score. Your credit score only looks into your financial status and overlooks all other qualitative aspects. Thus, it is important that you improve your credit score by improving your payment history, total debt owed, new credits, credit history and type of credit used.

5. These are the most important things that you should do if you want to improve your credit score. In the succeeding sections, there is a more in depth discussion on practical tips that you can use in order to improve your credit score and step-by-step DIY credit repair.

E. Improve Your Payment History

Aside from paying your debts to improve your credit score, it is important that you also work on improving your payment history. Payment history is defined as the record of your payment status in your credit report. This is an indication used by lenders and creditors as to whether you are capable of making timely payments.

As discussed in the previous section, your payment history contributes 35% on your credit score thus it is important that you do your best in improving your payment history. Below are some tips on how you can improve your payment history.

- Pay your bills regularly. Making delinquent payments can hurt your credit score even if you were late in making payment for a few days. Establish the habit of paying your bills early or on time.

- If you have missed a payment, make up for it by making regular payments for the following months. The longer you pay bills on time, the better your FICO score becomes. It is crucial to take note that older credit problems will not haunt your credit score forever as long as you make timely payments in the succeeding payment schedules.

- Contact your creditors or seek a credit counselor if you are having problems making ends meet. Your creditors may be more than willing to give you some leeway with your current payment plans.

These are some of the things that you can do in order to improve your payment history rating. However, after you have developed a discipline of making timely payments, it is important to take note that paying off your debts regularly will not really remove it from your credit report for seven years but it will improve your credit score nevertheless.

F. Lower Your Total Debt Owed

Another important factor in calculating the credit score is the total debt owed and it contributes to 30% of the FICO calculation. Improving the total debt owed means that you have to reduce the amount of your debt and this usually requires a lot of financial discipline on your part. Below are some important tips on how you can reduce your total debt owed.

- Keep your credit card debts low. One of the main reasons why people have bad credit scores is that they have high outstanding credit card debts. To reduce your total debt owed, you need to keep your credit card debts low. As much as possible, dedicate one year to lower your credit card debts by paying more than the minimum required payments.

- Pay off debts instead of moving them around. Some people apply for another credit card to pay off their current credit card debts. In reality, what they are mostly doing is moving their debts around. The best solution here is to dedicate your resources to paying off your debts and avoiding getting new credit cards until you have paid off your previous debts.

- Spend below your means. Spending below your means mean that you have to spend only on the basic things that you need. To raise your credit score, you need to avoid spending your money on things that you really do not need. Instead, dedicate most of your money to paying off your debts to improve your credit score.

- Create a budget. One of the best things that you can do to improve your total debt owed is to create a budget and stick to it. Sticking to your budget will allow you to prioritize your spending on what you only need.

G. Raise Your Credit Available

Most people and even uneducated credit professionals discuss your debt to income ratio. When you look at your credit report, your income is not listed. The debt to income ratio is not part of your credit report and cannot be calculated from your credit report. What most people are really referring to is your debt to your total credit lines. One way to make your debt look less significant is to lower this ratio with new credit lines that are lightly used, if used at all.

One thing you can do if you have just started to fix your credit is to slowly open new lines of credit with lenders that are easy to get credit from and who report to at least one of the credit reporting agencies.

To do this, go to a department store such as BestBuy, Home Depot or JC Pennies. These credit lines are reported to all three major reporting agencies and are easy to get. It may take a couple of months for them to show on your report, but rest assured the credit lines will get there.

When you get the card, buy something insignificant and pay off the card in short order.

H. Improve Your Length of Credit History

The length of credit history refers to the length of time of a person's credit history. Generally, a person needs to have 12 months of established credit history in order to borrow money. Looking at this factor is crucial because it allows lenders to gauge whether a particular individual has a good credit standing over a period of time. The credit history of an individual includes the following:

- Credit accounts from banks and loan companies
- Public records such as paid tax liens
- Collection accounts

Basically, the longer your length of credit history, the better it is for you to get a good credit score provided that you make regular payments to your debtor. Below are some tips on how you can improve your credit score by working on your length of credit history.

- If you have a short credit history, avoid opening too many new credit accounts. Opening many credit accounts will only lower your average account age which will have a big impact on your credit score. Moreover, building your credit too rapidly within a short period of time will make you look risky especially if you are a new credit user.

- Make regular payments to your creditors. Remember that bad credit information stays in your credit report for seven years for normal cases and 10 years for bankruptcy cases. If you have negative credit information, continue to make regular payments and make sure that you do not add more negative information in your credit report in the future. Let time heal your negative credit report.

Some people think that not having credit history is good but, contrary to this belief, not having a credit history will also make one questionable in the eyes of creditors and lenders. Take note that a credit history serves as the financial summary of a person and not having one will make it difficult for lenders and creditors to know if a particular person is capable of paying off debts or not.

I. New Credit

People who do not have credit history are often those who have not started working yet or are immigrant workers. In order to build their own credit history, they need to work on it in order to borrow funds. Generally, the best way to build a new credit is to apply for credit cards or apply for new loans. However, getting new credit cards can also put your credit score at risk especially if you do not make regular payments on time. For you to improve your credit score, here are some of the things that you can do:

- Do rate shopping for a particular loan. Search for a single loan and compare each rate for the same loan. Choose the loan that has amenable terms that you can keep up easily. By doing so, you will be able to manage your credit and make timely payments to improve your credit score.

o   Re-establish credit history that has problems. If your current credit history has problems, then you can open new accounts to raise your credit score. However, make sure that you make timely payments whenever you open new accounts.

o   Make sure to check your credit report whenever you open a new credit account or at some other interval you can stick to. That way, you will be able to manage your accounts wisely and keep track of the negative information on your credit report if any.

J. Types of Credit Use

Credits are used differently by different consumers. For some consumers, credit is used to pay for medical bills, house mortgage, car loans, as well as to pay for different kinds of purchases. When it comes to improving your credit score, make sure that you do the following:

o   Apply for new credit accounts when needed. Do not open accounts for the sake of diversifying your credits unless you are trying to raise your overall available credit. If you have self-control issues, you may not want to open any accounts unless absolutely needed.

o   Most people apply for credit accounts such as credit cards to pay for their purchases. However, it is important to take note that opening for new credit cards and not paying regularly can hurt their credit score. Manage your credit cards responsibly.

o   Closing a problematic credit account will not make your negative credit information go away. Some people think that closing a problematic credit account will not have any impact on their credit report. Instead of closing the account, find ways on how you can improve your credit score by settling your debts first.

K. Education Is Essential In DIY Credit Repair

Doing a DIY credit repair can take a lot of your time and energy but if you develop the discipline to improve your credit score, then you will find the task easy and worthwhile. By educating yourself, you will be able to figure out what your problem is and whether validating your debt or disputing it is your best option.

Education is also essential in DIY credit repair because it allows you to know your rights when it comes to your credit accounts. There are times when your creditors will pass the responsibility of collecting payments from you to debt collectors. If you do not educate yourself, you might become a hapless victim of harassment from aggressive debt collectors. For more on consumer's rights see Boiler's blog at NotLegalAdvice.org

L. Should You Do DIY Credit Repair or Hire a Company?

After reading about DIY credit repair in this chapter, now is the time to decide whether you should do DIY credit repair or not. Doing DIY credit repair has a lot of advantages but if you are a person who is unaware of the process of DIY credit repair, your best option is to seek help from a credit repair company to give you a jumpstart on what you needs to be done. DIY credit repair is a great option to save money on improving your credit repair but this option is not for everyone.

If you should decide to hire a credit repair company here is a checklist of questions we would ask them. You may not need to ask them all of the questions as some may not fit your particular situation.

Credit Repair company checklist:

Do you do:

1. Credit restoration
2. Credit building
3. Debt management & coaching
4. Student Loan rehabilitation
5. Collection Compliance and / or coaching
6. Loan origination coaching
7. Purchasing services (some credit services will actually help you buy a car, for example)
8. Security clearance services

9. Loan refinancing structuring and coaching

10. Accountability coaching

11. Budgeting coaching

Chapter 9
The Ethics of Credit Repair

All three of the authors of this book consider ethics to be of utmost importance. Everyone's ethics are of their own choice. Simply stated, whatever you decide to do, the authors of this book do not want you to compromise your ethics.

Disputing inaccuracies in your credit report is not only legal (see the FCRA), but also ethical. The FCRA states that the credit reporting agencies are required to maintain your report with 100% accuracy. Holding the credit reporting agencies to the federal law is ethical. Dispute all inaccuracies with all credit reporting agencies.

There is more of a debate on ethics when information is correct on your credit report. Is it really 100% correct?

Only one percent of accounts are 100% correct. When you look at your report, you will see a record of a department store and the amount you owe among other data. Look at the amount you owe. It may be $5204. There is never any "cents" added. What do you think the chances are of the balance being exactly zero cents? It is probably one in one hundred.

That may sound nitpicky, but consider if the tables were turned. What would the lender do if they could get out of a lawsuit on a technicality? We have yet to meet a corporate lawyer that wouldn't argue a technicality to get out of paying a bill or to get out of a lawsuit.

Another issue to consider is that we don't believe you owe a collection agency anything. If you have a debt with a bank and go into default, we believe you owe the bank money. If a collection agency buys that debt for 7 cents on the dollar without you agreeing to pay them, do you now owe them 100% of the debt? The most you could possibly owe them is what they paid for the debt. Anything above the 7% is legally called unjust enrichment.

Whatever you decide you have to sleep at night, so let your sense of ethics be your guide. We are pretty sure the bankers and financiers will sleep fine no matter what you decide.

Chapter 10
Insider's Secrets of Dispute Letters

We have sent tens of thousands of dispute letters. We have worked in management positions in the credit reporting agencies. We have spent years researching and using trial and error to improve this information over the years. As technology has improved, we have adapted.

Many others will claim that some of these ideas are just plain dumb. Before you believe them, ask them how many dispute letters they send a day.

We must admit, some of these tips sound crazy, but we have collected data over the years that suggest these methods are more effective than the other methods.

Here are the insider's secrets to disputing issues on your credit report. Understand these before you move on to the next chapter which is the recommended process.

1. Hand Write Your Letters

Handwrite all of your letters if you can write legibly. There are two big reasons for this.

All credit reporting agencies use a technology called OCR to scan your letters. OCR is optical character recognition software that is used to scan your letter. This software is dead on when it reads your typed letter. The software is not good at reading hand writing.

After your letter is normally scanned by OCR, the computer version of the letter is sent overseas for somebody overseas to decide if your dispute is valid. If you letter is handwritten, it cannot be OCRed and has to be read where it is sent. We have found that this is to your advantage.

Also, a hand written letter is clearly not mass produced and originated from a human. The credit reporting agencies aren't stupid. They can recognize mass produced dispute letters that people get online or sub-par software credit repair companies use. Most credit repair companies use software to print disputes. This software is used industry wide and creates similar letters. Companies that use software, such as Dispute Suit, to generate disputes on a printer will look much different than your hand written letter.

2. Hand Write Your Envelope and Use a Stamp

For similar reasons for hand writing your letters, hand write the envelope. Also use a regular stamp. Stamps.com and other letter postage printers are really convenient for other letters, but in this case, use a stamp.

3. Always Save a Copy

Always make a copy of everything you send to a credit reporting agency. Copy it after you sign the letter so that your copy is exactly what you sent them. One way is to start a file folder for each of the three credit reporting agencies. Every letter just gets filed in a folder.

Another method would be to scan every document you send and save it to a file folder. The key is to make sure this is backed up in case the computer gremlins strike.

Lawsuits are often won or lost on a person's ability to produce proof. You want to keep all letters to banks, collection agencies, credit reporting agencies and the like. You probably want to keep these forever.

4. Always Send a Copy of Two IDs with Correspondence

This may not technically be an insider secret. Almost all mediocre website and books on credit repair will tell you this. It bears repeating because it is true. Always send a copy of two IDs. If you don't do this, you will get what is called a "stall" letter stating that they need your ID. We generally send a copy of the driver's license and they work without fail. Here is a list of what you can use:

ID Docs Required by the Credit Reporting Agencies

Any One of the Following:
Driver's License
State ID Card
Passport
Military ID (Copy of Front and Back)

Proof of Current Mailing Address -Any Two of the Following:
Driver's License w/ Current Mailing Address

State ID Card w/ Current Mailing Address
Utility Bills —Water, Gas, Electric, Cable TV/Satellite TV or Telephone (Cell Phone Bills not Accepted)
Bank or Credit Union Statement (Credit Card Statements not Accepted)
Cancelled Check — Front and Back (Voided Checks not Accepted)
Government Issued ID Card
Paycheck Stub with Name and Address
Signed Letter from Homeless Shelter
Stamped PO Box Receipt

*Make sure that utility bills, bank statements (or cancelled checks) and paycheck stubs are recent and must be less than 2 months old. A bank statement and cancelled check on the same account is only one proof of residence.

*All state issued license and identification cards must be current and unexpired.

*Electronic statements printed from a website cannot be accepted for proof of address.

Proof Of SSN - Any One of the Following:
Social Security Card
Copy of a Recent W2, 1099 or Declaration Page of Tax Return
Military ID (Copy of Front and Back)

5. Send Certified Mail

This is optional. If you think there is the potential that you are going to sue the credit reporting agency, you want to send your letter certified. You do not need the return receipt unless you want it.

Under normal situations it is not necessary to send certified mail. Most of the time you send a dispute you will get a letter back from the credit reporting agency. If you want proof that you sent the dispute because you suspect you will have an FCRA lawsuit or a similar issue, then absolutely use certified mail. It will be worth the extra few dollars to have proof.

6. Always Use the US Mail to Dispute

There are three methods of disputing accounts on your credit reports: Written, online and the phone. We much prefer good old US mail because it leaves a paper trail if you follow the steps above. If your credit report issues get nasty, you will be glad you have papers to prove your side of the story.

Insider's Secrets of What NOT to Do

1. Never Make a Payment on Disputed Debt

Often the advice you get from people, even those who should know better, is to negotiate all of your debts to lower the amount you owe. While this seems like a common sense solution, it will often make your credit situation worse, your credit score may drop, at make your bad credit last longer.

2. Reaging Your Debt

Normally, a bad debt will stay on your credit report for 7 years. This is a generalization based on your last payment. Legally, it is more accurate to say seven years plus 180 days is how long a negative can stay on your report. For simplification, let's just say seven years.

If you made a payment on a credit on a credit card six and a half years ago, it can be on your credit report for another half year. If you make a payment now, it will reset the clock and the account can be on your credit report until seven years from your new payment. You just added six and a half years of having this on your account by making a payment. Don't let this happen to you. Collection companies know that accounts that are six and a half years past the last payment are not worth suing over.

3. Never Admit the Debt

When debts are disputed, it is the debtor's burden to prove the debt. Don't do their job by admitting the debt. By admitting the debt, you will virtually lose many of your rights protected by federal laws. Federal laws protect you from collector's actions and are not usually about the debt. As odd as it sounds, it is difficult to defend your rights after you have admitted the debt. You are done.

It is perfectly ethical, in our opinion, to not admit the debt, but say something like," I don't know". Do you really know if the debt is yours and can admit the amount of the debt without seeing your signature on an application and seeing a complete accounting of the account since its inception?

One last thing to note about admitting the debt is that collectors have a trick to get you to do this. They will try to get you to make a good faith payment of $1. They will say that they cannot investigate your account without a small offering to show their boss or somebody that you are serious about this. Don't fall for it. If it is not your account, or it is in dispute don't give them a cent.

If you make any payment you agree to the debt. It will be almost impossible to argue a debt you have been making payments towards.

Chapter 11
Step-by-Step Do It Yourself Credit Repair

Note: the following method is based on the ethical perspective stated in the previous chapter. Adjust your plan accordingly.

1. Obtain Your Credit Report

Obtain your credit report from the big three credit reporting agencies. Make sure they are less than 30 days old when you begin this process. If you are close to the 30 day limit, get going on the next steps.

2. Dispute Personal Information

Write a letter to all three credit agencies disputing all old addresses, old phone numbers, old employers, other names listed. If it has your spouse listed, dispute the spouse. You may not want to tell your spouse that they are in dispute; I will leave that up to you.

Here is what your dispute letter will look like. Please use your own words.

Date

Experian
P.O. Box 4500
Allen, TX 75013

Your Name
Your Address

Dear Experian,

I received a copy of my Experian credit report on (date). There are some inaccuracies in my personal information that I believe you are required to correct.

One page 17:
You have the following names on my account. My name is William Smith, I have never been known as or called Billy Smith, Willie Smith. Please remove these from my file as they are not me.

On Page 19:

I have never lived at 123 Main Street. Remove the address from my file.

Also on page 19:

You have a spouse listed for me. Mary Smith is not my spouse.

Your prompt attention to these details is appreciated.

Sincerely,
William Smith
Date of Birth 10/20/1952

The reason you want to eliminate all of your old personal data is simple. When you dispute an account, the less information the credit reporting agency has on you, the less likely they are to verify your old accounts.

After you send this dispute letter there is nothing to do until you get the results back from the credit reporting agencies.

When you get the results back, if all of the disputed items are removed move on to the next step. If not send the letters out one more time. After the second letter gets a reply move on to the second step with or without the information being removed.

3. Round 1 - Dispute All Negative Information

The next thing to do is dispute all negative information on your credit reports. Limit your letter to six issues at a time. Send the disputes to all three credit reporting agencies.

Your letters need to be in your words following the guidelines in Chapter 10. Here is an example:

Your name
Address

Credit Reporting Agency
Address (See Chapter 2, section E)

Date

Dear Experian,

I am in receipt of my credit report that you sent me. I received it on December, 6th 2013.

I am shocked to see the following alleged accounts on my consumer report:

Macys, Account # 123456, balance: $1345
Chase Visa, Account #1234567, Balance $4502
GMAC, Account # 345678, Balance $34692

These accounts are not mine. Please remove these accounts immediately.

Sincerely, Your Name

Keep this letter simple and don't seem too smart. This is not the time to let them know that you have a plan and are going to clean your credit.

Remember to attach your ID as described in Chapter 10. Also, attach a copy of your credit report with the disputed trade lines highlighted or underlined. Send certified as described in Chapter 10 too.

After you have sent out this round of letters, you have to wait for the Credit Reporting Agencies to respond. If they respond and remove all of the items you disputed, congratulations, you are done. If not, move on to Round Two.

4. Round 2 – Send Them a Mildly Threatening Letter

The next round of letters needs to be somewhat threatening. The normal approach is to bring up the FTC. We believe that the FTC is a toothless government agency that will do you little good in reality. The threat of the FTC is often enough to get the credit reporting agency to delete your disputed trade lines. He is a sample of a round two letter:

Your name
Address

Credit Reporting Agency
Address (See Chapter 2, section E)

Date

Dear Experian,

I was quite shocked that you claimed to verify the alleged debts that disputed on (date).

For your reference, the incorrect debts are:

Macys, Account # 123456, balance: $1345
Chase Visa, Account #1234567, Balance $4502
GMAC, Account # 345678, Balance $34692

As you can imagine, I was dismayed that you claimed to have verified debt that is not mine. I called the FTC to file a complaint. They thought I should give you one more chance before filing an official complaint. This is my last attempt to clear this up before filing an official complaint.

As I stated before, these accounts are not mine. Please remove these accounts immediately.

Sincerely, Your Name

Then, send a letter to the alleged original creditor. This will be a similar letter:

Your name
Address

Creditor
Address (look it up online)

Date

Dear Chase Bank,

I was quite shocked that you claimed to verify the alleged debts that disputed on (date).

For your reference, the incorrect debt is:

Chase Visa, Account #1234567, Balance $4502

As you can imagine, I was dismayed that you claimed to have verified debt that is not mine. I called the FTC to file a complaint. They thought I should give you one more chance before filing an official complaint. This is my last attempt to clear this up before filing an official complaint.

Please send me the information that you used to verify this account. Since this is not my account, this information will be erroneous.

As I stated before, these accounts are not mine. Please remove these accounts from my credit reports immediately.

Sincerely, Your Name

Again, you are waiting for responses after you send these letters. At this stage, you may need to send a few variations of these letters claiming to be close to hiring legal representation or whatever you can come up with and are comfortable saying.

5. Round 3 – Consumer Financial Protection Bureau

As we state in the last section, we believe that the FTC is essentially worthless in helping Americans who are having trouble with collectors or a credit reporting agency. We stand by this statement.

Although the FTC is ineffective, don't give up on the government to help you. The Consumer Financial Protection Bureau (CFPB) was established by the Dodd–Frank Wall Street Reform and Consumer Protection Act signed into law by President Obama in July 2010. The CFPB is an independent unit located inside and funded by the United States Federal Reserve. This sounds bad, right?

In reality this is a new government agency and so far our results and our feedback have been excellent. If you still have issues on your credit report, file a complaint with the CFPB. There are three ways you can file a CFPB complaint.

You can call them at (855) 411-2372 to file a complaint by phone. We do not recommend this as there is no paper trail for you. It is also much more difficult to explain the situation without getting emotional.

You can file a complaint on-line. This is the fastest way to file a complaint. You will be able to upload any supporting documentation you have. To file a complaint on-line go to:

http://www.consumerfinance.gov/complaint/

Lastly you can send the CFPB an old fashioned letter. This is what we recommend and have great results doing. Send a neat formal letter explaining the situation. Attach all documentation. Make sure you explain the outcome you desire. This is a sample of a letter that was sent to the CFPB and got a negative trade line off of a client's credit report:

Your name
Address

Consumer Financial Protection Bureau
P.O. Box 4503
Iowa City, Iowa 52244

Date

Dear Consumer Financial Protection Bureau,

I have a debt on my credit report that is not mine. I have written Experian, Equifax and TransUnion to dispute the debt. I have disputed with them three times each (see attached dispute letters). I have also written Chase Bank directly twice (see attached).

For your reference, the incorrect debts are:

Chase Visa, Account #1234567, Balance $4502

I would like to formally file a complaint against Chase Bank, Experian, Equifax and TransUnion for putting false information on my credit reports.

My hope is that by filing this complaint, that all 3 credit reporting agencies will remove this trade line from my credit report.

Let me know if there is further documentation or information that will aid your investigation.

Sincerely, Your Name

Wait for the results of this letter. If this removes the issue, congratulations... If this does not clear the trade line from your credit report, proceed to the next step.

6. Round 4 – Get Help

It has been our experience that the first two steps (or rounds) will eliminate most of the negative trade lines on your credit reports. It is some work and takes some time, but you have likely cleared most, if not all of your issues.

If you have not cleared all of your negative trade lines, you are going to have to make a choice on what to do next.

We apologize, but some of this section will sound like a sales pitch. These are the solutions we have found and are willing to help you if you reach out to us. There are others you can reach out to as well, but we can't speak to their results.

If you check your credit score now, you score may have improved enough at this point that you do not care about what is actually on the report. This could be the case if your goal is to buy a car. Car dealers usually only look at your credit score to make their loan decisions. If your goal is to buy a house, the negative credit lines are much more likely to be noticed and hurt your loan rates or approval.

It is unlikely that you have worked to this point and have serious credit problems, but sometimes there is an item that just won't come off of your credit report. At this point you have three last resorts. You can hire a lawyer to sue the original creditor or the credit reporting agencies. You can learn how to sue them without a lawyer. Lastly, you can hire a credit repair company.

Hiring a lawyer can be tricky. It has been our experience that most lawyers know nothing about credit report issues and the Fair Credit Reporting Act. We have only worked with a handful of lawyers that can handle the job. If you would like a referral, please feel free to call Brad at National Credit Solutions. Brad can likely refer you to a lawyer that will charge you nothing to represent you. The contact information is listed at the end of this book.

Another avenue to keep fighting your credit report issues is to sue the debtor or credit reporting agencies without a lawyer. When you are in litigation without a lawyer, it is called being "Pro Se". This sounds incredibly difficult. It is not difficult and it is really empowering when you win. A good place to start your research is Boiler's website NotLegalAdvice.org

Lastly, you could hire a credit repair company. We have already shared our ideas with you on this process. If you are this far along it is likely that you passed on hiring a credit repair company and decided to strike out on your own. It might be time to revisit that decision. If you only have a single negative trade line on your credit report, you are in a great position to negotiate when you now hire a credit report company.

Chapter 12
Final Thoughts

It probably took you some time to make the credit mess you are in. Getting out of the mess is going to take some time as well. You need to stick with it and be methodical about your credit recovery.

The three authors of this book have helped thousands of people in situations similar to your's. We did our best to share our advice with you. We focused on the information that we believe most people with credit issues need to know.

The reason we wrote this book was to help people like you. If you have questions or need more information, feel free to reach out to one or all of us. We are here to help.

We wish you success in your credit improvement plan and in life.

About Boiler

Boiler Williams grew up in Indiana and went to Purdue University. He continued his education in Denver at Regis University. At Regis he earned a master's degree in Computer science and a few years later he earned a MBA.

While working his way through college, Boiler became a stanch consumer rights advocate and began helping people with credit report issues and collection issues. He continues as a consumer rights advocate to this day.

Boiler fights the largest debt collectors in the country. He generally sues them in Federal Court without a lawyer. He has not lost a case in court yet. He has sued debt collectors for their multiple violations of the Fair Debt Collection Practices Act (FDCPA) and the Fair Credit Reporting Act (FCRA). Boiler has pending litigation for collectors' violation of the Telephone Consumer Protection Act (TCPA) that will likely commence in 2014.

Boiler has written a #1 Amazon book on doing legal research on the federal court's Pacer system. This eBook can be found on Amazon.com here.

Contact Boiler

Email: boiler@NotLegalAdvice.org

Website: www.NotLegalAdvice.org

Facebook: https://www.facebook.com/notlegaladvice

About Brad

Brad Boruk started out his professional career selling cars; he was obsessed with customer satisfaction. Brad understood that customer satisfaction made people happy and it also sent him referral business.

After becoming a top salesperson based on his ability to make customers happy, Brad noticed a problem with the industry, people with no credit or bad credit were treated differently, and they were not treated fairly. The next logical step for him was to learn the credit industry inside and out so that he could help his customers get good deals.

As Brad learned more about the credit side of business he realized that this was what interested him; helping people with credit. He changed his career from selling cars to helping people with credit and other personal finance matters.

In 2007 Brad started National Credit Solutions; his goal was to help people realize their dreams. Some people dream of owning their first new car, others dream of owning their first home for their family, yet others dream of starting their own business. Year after year Brad and his company have helped these people realize their dreams through credit and money management.

Brad is excited about writing books to share his practical knowledge. Brad is currently the author of this short book "A Guide to Your Financial Health: How to Budget and How to Get More from Your Money" where he helps people with budgeting and savings. His latest project is working with Boiler Williams on an insider's guide to consumer credit. This project is ongoing.

Contact Brad

Brad Boruk

c/o National Credit Solutions

2035 Central Circle Suite 110
McKinney, TX 7506

Direct Dial: 214-504-7100

Email: info@NCS700.com

Website: www.NCS700.com

About Ray

Ray Clark enjoys many hobbies and disciplines. He considers himself a renaissance man in that he is open to and willing to learn any subject or activity. His employment path has taken him through loans and credit. He has even worked with one of the major credit bureaus in the United States to help educate people on the nature of credit reporting.

At one point in his career path, he started helping people understand and learn how to recover from financial and credit follies. Taking his own personal experiences and those from his various employment endeavors he desired to share some of that with you.

If you enjoyed this book, you may enjoy these as well:

A Guide to Your Financial Health: How to Budget And How to Get More from Your Money **by Brad Boruk, Ray Clark and Boiler Williams**

Pro Se Guide To Using And Understanding Pacer.gov **by** Boiler Williams **and Brad Boruk**

Hidden Credit Repair Secrets - Extreme Version (Third Edition) **by Clayborne, Mark**

You Need A Budget **by** Jesse Mecham

CPSIA information can be obtained at www.ICGtesting.com
Printed in the USA
LVOW11s1355210215

427802LV00001B/107/P